50 GEMS

West Cork

KIERAN McCARTHY

AMBERLEY

CW00556815

Dedicated to my parents, Eleanor and John, and holidays in West Cork

First published 2019

Amberley Publishing
The Hill, Stroud
Gloucestershire, GL5 4EP

www.amberley-books.com

Copyright © Kieran McCarthy, 2019

The right of Kieran McCarthy to be identified as the Author
of this work has been asserted in accordance with the
Copyrights, Designs and Patents Act 1988.

All rights reserved. No part of this book may be reprinted
or reproduced or utilised in any form or by any electronic,
mechanical or other means, now known or hereafter invented,
including photocopying and recording, or in any information
storage or retrieval system, without the permission in writing
from the Publishers.

British Library Cataloguing in Publication Data.
A catalogue record for this book is available from the British Library.

ISBN 978 1 4456 9239 5 (paperback)
ISBN 978 1 4456 9240 1 (ebook)

Typesetting by Aura Technology and Software Services, India.
Printed in Great Britain.

Contents

Acknowledgements

I would like to sincerely thank the commissioning and editorial staff at Amberley Publishing for continuing to put their faith in my books and for the valuable advice and assistance they always provide. I would like to thank the hard-working staff of Cork City and Cork County Libraries for their help. I would like to express my gratitude to Mairéad, my parents, my family and public supporters for continually challenging me to think about the importance of heritage in a bigger, macro picture.

Introduction

There were two words – raw and epic – which constantly came to mind as my 400cc scooter motorcycle traversed the roads and byways of West Cork while researching this book. Both came to mind as I felt almost swallowed up on my small bike, disappearing on routeways that duck and weave through hollowed-out rock scarred by glaciation movements for 20,000 years or parked up on coastal beaches where the folding of the rock, derived from near the origins of the universe, can be seen. This book builds on a previous publication called *West Cork Through Time* (Amberley Publishing, 2015), which explored the fascination of postcard makers 100 years ago with its scenery, its culture and its people. This book returns to some of those sites previously chosen and new ones, exploring how those key sites became the focus of attention and development, and how their stories, memories and the making of new narratives were articulated in an attempt to preserve an identity and/or communities locally and nationally at sites or to create new identities and communities. For example, several sites in this book came into being in the fledging years of the Irish Free State where tourism and story-telling about the nation's history was highlighted or some sites were created from the burgeoning boom time of 1960s Ireland, where the focus was on developing industry and recreational amenities.

The book explores fifty well-known gems of the West Cork region. It brings their stories together in an accessible manner. It is not meant to provide a full history of a site but perhaps does try to provide new lenses through which heritage is looked at to explore the power of narrative construction and collective memory in West Cork. The book takes the reader from Bandon to Dursey Island, from Gougane Barra to the Healy Pass.

Researching West Cork, the visitor discovers that each parish has its own local historian, historical society, village council, sometimes a library, tidy town's group, community group and business community, which have inspired the collection of stories, the creation of heritage trails and information panels, and have championed a strong sense of place and identity. Relics from the past also haunt the landscape, with prominent landmarks ranging from Bronze Age standing stones to ivy-clad ruined houses and castles, churches and old big houses, to beacons, cable cars and lighthouses. All add to the narrative of the spectacle that is West Cork.

While attempts have been made at compiling local histories in West Cork, there is a need to compile the macro historical picture of West Cork. Certainly, the work of Fáilte Ireland's Wild Atlantic Way has been key in bringing many threads of stories together, kickstarting long-forgotten traditions and empowering communities to present their story to the visitor. In particular this book draws on the brilliant Irish Newspaper Archive where the past editions of the *Cork Examiner* and the *Southern Star* are digitised and provide much information at different points of a site's evolution. Looking closely at the human detail of a building, statue or view can reveal nuances about how places are seen and understood and ultimately can be championed going forward into the future.

Kieran McCarthy

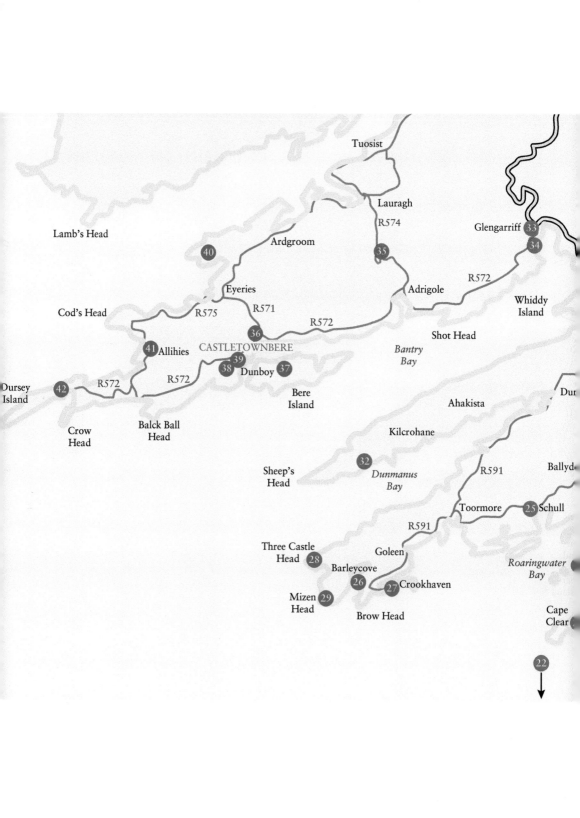

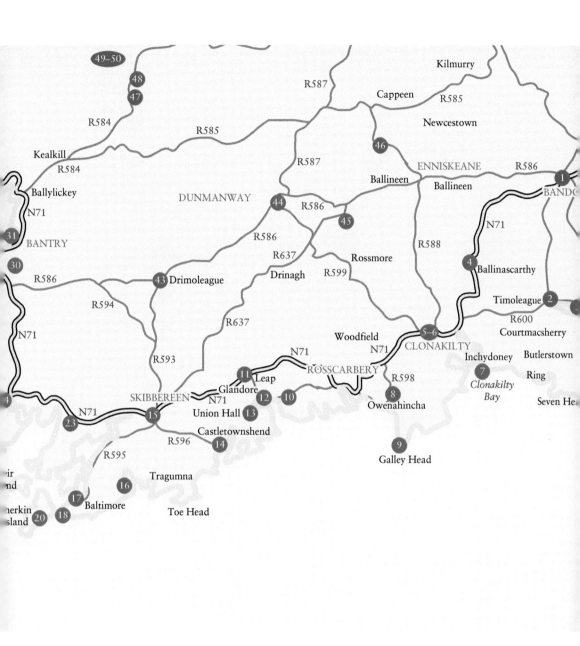

1. The Capture of the Past – Bandon and its Bridge

The origins of the towns of West Cork can vary from medieval times to the early twentieth century. On walking around them what is particularly impressive is the nineteenth-century fabric, which makes for very photogenic spaces to capture. There are old and colourful shopfronts, old narrow laneways and streets, ornate water pumps, cobbled surfaces, historic marketplaces, eye-catching churches, as well as 200-year-old bridges and bridges even older than this. These latter traits define the look of, and layer with stories, much of West Cork's towns. For example, on a sunny day as the sun sets, the colourful shopfronts of Bandon's Main Street with its stone-built fabric bridge are illuminated.

Bandon derives its name from the erection of a bridge over the River Bandon and owes its origin to the English planters on the great Desmond forfeitures in the reign of Elizabeth. In 1609, James I granted to Henry Beecher the privilege of a Saturday market and two fairs at the town. Power was given to him and his heirs to appoint a clerk of the market in the newly erected town of Bandon-Bridge, or in any other town within the territory, with the privilege of licensing all tradesmen and artisans settling in them.

The grants were purchased shortly afterwards by Richard Boyle, the 1st Earl of Cork, whose efforts in promoting the town's growth and prosperity led him to rewrite history as such and to be regarded as the founder of the town. He peopled it with a colony of Protestant merchants from Bristol and established iron-smelting and

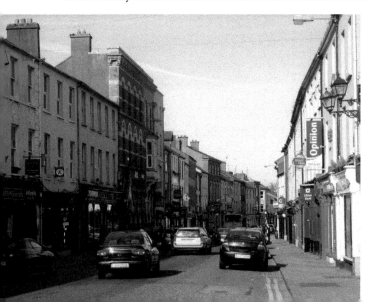

Main Street, Bandon.

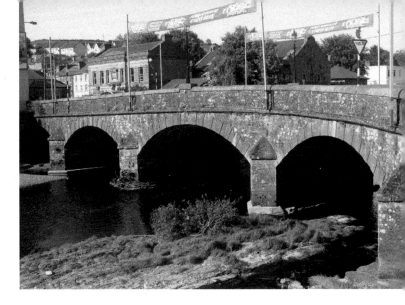

Bandon Bridge,
Bandon.

linen-weaving industries, all of which in a few short years flourished and increased in extent and importance. The manufacture of camlets, stuffs, and other woollen goods prevailed in Bandon to the close of the eighteenth century and the beginning of the nineteenth and was succeeded by the spinning and weaving of cotton, which continued to flourish until 1825. Spinning mills were then erected on a large scale, and more than 1,000 people were employed in weaving.

In the early seventeenth century, Bandon was under continuous attack by dispossessed Irish native families such as the O'Mahonys. Subsequently, in 1620 Richard Boyle began the construction of a wall around the town. The wall took approximately five years to build and enclosed an area of 27 acres.

The town walls were taken down as the eighteenth century progressed (sections of the town wall can still be traced). What has survived is a bridge on the site of the original Bandon Bridge. A construction date of 1778 is on the western parapet and on the eastern parapet an enlargement date of 1838 is highlighted on a plaque. Both plaques highlight investment by local landlords and the British parliament in maintaining and opening up new road networks. Apart from its layered past, the bridge also remains as a marker to remind the visitor to also look at the detail of the infrastructure of the West Cork region and how it helped link some very beautiful towns and their respective stories.

2. The Lure of the Past – Timoleague Franciscan Abbey

The lure of the ruinous Timoleague Abbey is too difficult to resist. Here one enters a maze of stone-walled rooms and headstones emerging from the ground from all angles. The abbey is a remnant of the early phase of Old English colonisation and remains one of the most impressive ruins of an abbey in the south of Ireland.

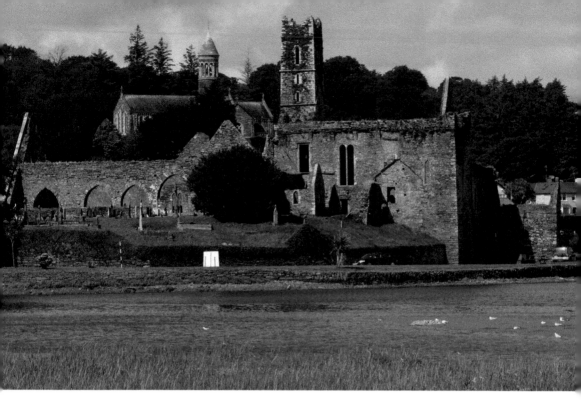

Timoleague Abbey, adjacent to the Ilen River.

Following the Anglo-Norman invasion of 1169 large parts of Ireland were colonised. Anglo-Norman families such as the Barrys and the Hodnetts settled in this area and their surnames and placenames survive to the present day. In the thirteenth century, a great battle was fought at Timoleague between the Hodnetts and the Barrys. Lord Philip Hodnett, the leader of the Hodnetts, was killed, and Irishmen routed by the Barrys under Lord Barrymore. The latter and his descendants then became the owners of Barryroe and the district around Timoleague. A member of the Hodnetts became Gaelicised and began to use the Irish form 'Seafraidh'. His descendants became MacSeafraidh and from their court or castle, the name Cúirt Mhic Sheafraidh or anglicised Courtmacsherry.

Local folklore and secondary historical accounts show a range of dates, but it looks like it was at least founded between 1240 and 1316 by either Donal Glas MacCarthy or William de Barry. St Mologa, after whom the abbey was called, was a native of Fermoy district in the seventh century AD.

The remains of the abbey consist of a church with ranges of domestic buildings around a cloister to the north. A walk through the buildings shows considerable alterations as the structure developed to take in new buildings. For example, the tall narrow tower in the church is an inserted feature as it blocks window embrasures in the north and south walls of the choir.

There are several tombs of old Irish families of distinction to be found within its walls. Here lie the McCarthy-Reaghs of nearby Kilbrittain Castle and also the tombs of the De Courceys of Kinsale. Bishop Egan was killed in a battle with the English, near Bandon, in 1601. In this fight the Irish were defeated, but carried off the bishop's body from the field and buried it with episcopal and military honour at Timoleague. After Timoleague friary was plundered by English forces in 1612 it

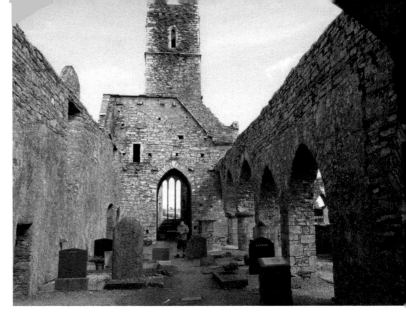

Interior of
Timoleague Abbey.

began to be used as a burial ground by local people. In the sacristy there is also a stone with a circular depression known as wart well.

Brother Micheal O'Cleirigh, chief of the quartet that produced the *Annals of the Four Masters,* during his progress around Ireland, collecting and copying monastic documents. The famous Book of Lismore was kept here in the abbey's library and O'Cleirigh studied it.

The preservation of Timoleague Abbey in the eighteenth century is mainly due to the care bestowed on it by the Travers family and the Office of Public Works in the late nineteenth century, twentieth century and early twenty-first century, as well as various local community preservation committees.

3. A Guardian of the Seas – Courtmacsherry Lifeboat Station

The history of the Courtmacsherry Lifeboat Station is a gem for reasons of heroism and guardianship. In 1824 the Royal National Lifeboat Institution was established. A year later, two of the first lifeboat stations in Cork were established in Courtmacsherry and Kinsale respectively. The first record of a lifeboat in Cork Harbour also dates back as far back as 1825. In 1858, the Ballycotton Station was established by the RNLI to ensure a safe passage for shipping visiting the port of Cork. During this time new stations also appeared at Youghal and Ardmore. The Queenstown Lifeboat Station was established by the institution in 1866 following several wrecks with loss of life off Cork Harbour.

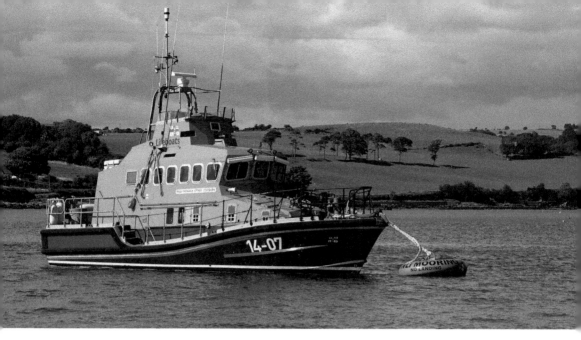

Courtmacsherry Lifeboat moored in Courtmacsherry Bay.

Stories abound across local newspapers of the activities of the Courtmacsherry lifeboat through the years of the lives saved and the ones who unfortunately were not rescued. For example, on the evening of 20 July 1900 a large steamer was reported in distress in Seven Heads Bay. The weather at the time was foggy; there was no wind and the sea was smooth. At 6 p.m. the lifeboat *Farrant* proceeded to assist of the vessel and found her to be the *Texan* from Liverpool, bound for St Thomas, with a general cargo, and having about 200 persons on board. She had a large hole amidship, having been in collision with another steamer in the fog. The lifeboat remained by her until two steam tugs arrived from Queenstown and took her in tow.

During the First World War, RNLI lifeboat crews launched 1,808 times, rescuing 5,332 people. With many younger men on active service, the average age of a lifeboatman was over fifty. Many launches were to ships that had been torpedoed or struck mines, including naval or merchant vessels on war duty and many were in non-motor propelled boats. The *Lusitania*, on route to New York on 7 May 1915, was torpedoed and sunk by a German U-boat south of Courtmacsherry Bay, with the loss of 1,201 lives. The Courtmacsherry Lifeboat crew was alerted to the tragedy and, because of very fine weather that day, the sails were of no use so they rowed the heavy *Kezia Gwilt* lifeboat 15 miles, or for four hours, to the scene of the sinking.

A midnight rescue by of Courtmacsherry Lifeboat was witnessed at Garretstown Bay on 9 December 1932 when the three-masted auxiliary schooner *Elizabeth Drew* of New Ross, storm-bound and practically dismantled, drifted off the rock-riddled shore. She ran into a gale in mid-channel, which blew her off her course, flooded the forecastle, wrecked the galley, and carried away the foresails. Rockets were sent up and the Courtmacsherry Lifeboat, which had already been communicated with by the lighthouse keeper on the Old Head, went out under Coxwain Bulpin. After an hour's battle in the teeth of the north-easterly gale she got alongside the crippled schooner and assisted her to Courtmacsherry.

In 1998, a new two-storey boathouse replaced an old building to host a twenty-five-man crew. It was built on the exact site of the old boathouse, which was

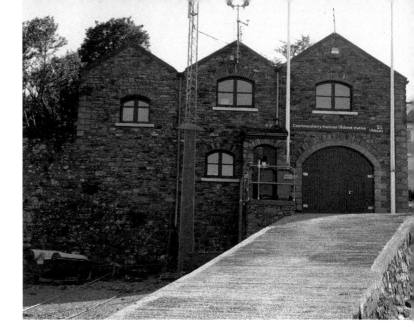

Courtmacsherry
Lifeboat Station.

built in 1929. The new boathouse included a large room for launching the lifeboat's punt used by the crew to get out to the £125 million Trent Class Lifeboat, *Frederick Storey Cockburn*, which Courtmacsherry took delivery of in 1995. Today there are forty-five lifeboat stations in Ireland and 237 in total run by the Royal National Lifeboat Institution.

The year 1998 also coincided with the launch of the Seven Heads walk, which extends from Timoleague village through Courtmacsherry, around the rugged cliffs and shoreline towards Dunworley Bay and on to Barryscove, Ardgehane and Ballinglanna.

4. An Industrial Inheritance – Ballinascarty's Model T Ford Sculpture

Halfway between Bandon and Clonakilty lies a wonderful silver monument of a Model T Ford. In September 2000 Edwin Nolan, chairman and managing director of Henry Ford & Son Ltd, unveiled the monument. The sculpture commemorates the fact that it was from Ballinascarty that Henry Ford's father emigrated in 1847 for Dearborn, Michigan, where the Ford Motor Company was later founded. The monument, a life-size stainless steel replica of the famous car, affectionately known as the 'Tin Lizzie', was sculpted by artist Kevin Holland.

Henry Ford's grandfather John was a native of Wolfe Tone Street in Cork City. In later life, he moved with his family to become tenants on an estate at Ballinascarty, near Bandon. John had three brothers, Samuel, Henry and George, who emigrated to America in search of fortune in the 1830s. During the height of the Great Famine in 1847, John Ford left Ireland for the US also in search of fortune. In his emigrant party, which included his mother, his wife Thomasina, their seven sons and his brothers' family, was John Ford's son, William, who had been born in 1826. The Ford family eventually settled in Michigan and in 1848, John Ford bought an 80-acre farm at Dearborn in Michigan. His son, William, having spent some years helping to extend the Michigan Central Railway westward to Lake Michigan, took a job on the farm of Patrick Ahern in the town of Dearborn. Here, William met and married Mary Litogot, Ahern's foster daughter, and bought his own farm at Dearborn. The first child was stillborn, but on 30 July 1863, Mary gave birth to a son whom they named Henry.

In 1891, Ford became an engineer with the Edison Illuminating Company in Detroit. This event signified a conscious decision on Ford's part to dedicate his life to industrial pursuits. His promotion to chief engineer in 1893 gave him enough time and money to devote attention to his personal experiments on internal combustion engines. These experiments culminated in 1896 with the completion of his own self-propelled vehicle – the Quadricycle.

After two unsuccessful attempts to establish a company to manufacture automobiles, the Ford Motor Company was incorporated in June 1903 with Henry Ford as vice-president and chief engineer. Henry Ford realized his dream of producing an automobile that was reasonably priced, reliable and efficient with the introduction of the Model T in 1908. This vehicle initiated a new era in personal transportation.

Sculpture of Model T Ford by artist Kevin Holland.

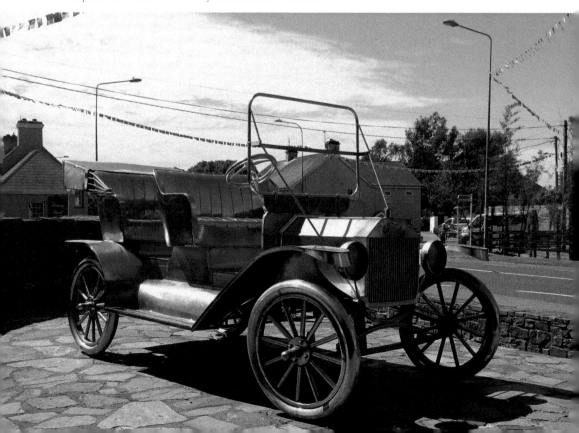

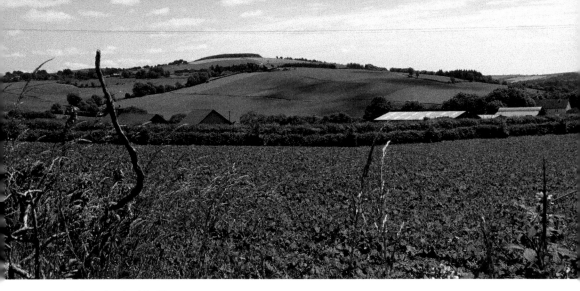

Townland of Ballinascarty.

It was easy to operate, maintain and handle on rough roads, immediately becoming a huge success. From 1908 to 1927, the company would sell more than 15 million Model T cars and trucks in the US and Europe.

In November 1916, Fords made an offer to purchase the freehold of the Cork Park Grounds and considerable land adjoining the river near the Marina in Cork City. Ford, Cork Corporation and the Cork Harbour Commissioners entered into formal negotiations. The plant being laid down by the company was specially designed for the manufacture of an Agricultural Motor Tractor, well known as the 'fordson', a 22-horse power, four-cylinder tractor, working with kerosene or paraffin, adaptable either for ploughing or as a portable engine arranged for driving machinery by belt drive. The Cork factory was to provide 'fordsons' to local, regional and national farmers and further afield on the Continent.

5. Ashlin's Delight – Clonakilty and Its Church Heritage

Clonakilty was formally founded in 1613 by Richard Boyle when he received a charter from James I. It appears to have replaced the nearby medieval settlement of Kilgarriff as the focus for urban development. Established as a market town, in time it was engaged chiefly in the manufacture of linen and cotton through its elaborate mills. Breweries were developed in the eighteenth century and corn and potatoes were exported to Cork. The present town was largely laid out in the period 1788–1840.

In the late nineteenth century, the Bishop of Cork Dr William Delaney and his successor Dr Thomas O'Callaghan pursued a vast building programme to replace the primitive churches of the diocese with new iconic edifices for veneration. Up to 1880 the Roman Catholic community of Clonakilty were baptized and prayed in the little

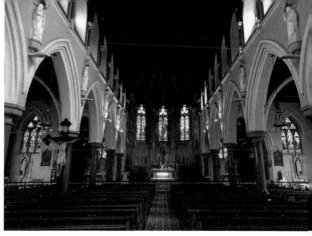

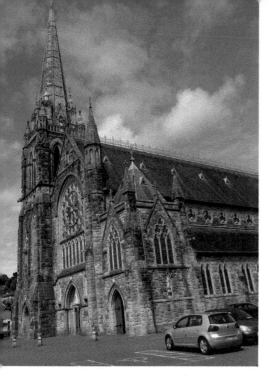

Above: Wolfe Tone Street, Clonakilty.

Left: Church of the Immaculate Conception, Clonakilty.

church on Western Road where the former boys' national school now stands. A new cathedral-sized church called Church of the Immaculate Conception was opened on 25 July 1880 close to the site of the old church after ten years of building work. The task of building this church was undertaken by Fr Matthew O'Donovan when he was appointed parish priest of Clonakilty in 1868. He never saw it completed, however, as he died in 1875. It was designed in the Gothic Revival style by architect George Ashlin (1837–1921) and is built of green sandstone, which was quarried locally, with tracings of county Wicklow granite. The spire was erected in the 1890s and the bell was installed in 1898.

Between 1856 and 1889 George had been involved in the design of several key Roman churches in the Cork region. An experienced architect, in 1856 George became a pupil of Edward Welby Pugin. Many commissions followed, almost all of them for Catholic churches, convents and monasteries throughout the country, culminating in the new cathedral at Queenstown (Cobh), Co. Cork. The partnership of Pugin & Ashlin was dissolved in the latter months of 1868. However, by this time George had seen involvement in church projects such as in Ardfert, County Kerry, dedicated in 1868, Brosna Church began to be built in 1869 as well as Ballyroe Church in County Cork in 1869, and the foundation stone of Carrigtwohill church laid in 1869.

George Ashlin's plan for Clonakilty consisted of a nave, aisle, transepts, a chancel and a baptistry. The stones of the spire were dowelled into one another, each section being put together at ground level by the firm John Sisk & Sons at Cork before being moved to Clonakilty by train. The bell was mounted in 1898 and is cast from the Fountain Head Bell Foundry in Dublin. The fine interior retains much of its outstanding fabric intact. Renovations during the 1990s have restored the interior of the church to its former splendour. The church comprises a nave, aisles, transepts, two chapels and a baptistry. The altar of the Sacred Heart was erected by James Pearse of Dublin (father of Pádraig Pearse, patriot and leader of the 1916 Rising) at a cost of £350. The approximate cost for the erection of the church was £36,000.

6. The Landscapes of a Statesman – Remembering Michael Collins

The commemorative landscapes of Michael Collins are all gems to explore in the Clonakilty area. Born in Clonakilty in 1890, Michael Collins in his early years was inspired at his national school at Lisvair by his teacher Denis Lyons, who was a member of the Irish Republican Brotherhood (IRB). Stories abounded of rebellion and the various stands against British imperial control. In 1906 Michael emigrated to England and worked as a postal clerk in the civil service. During this time, he participated in Irish organisations such as the Gaelic League, which promoted the use of the Irish language. The writings of Arthur Griffith and his work in establishing Sinn Féin inspired Michael to become a member of the IRB and later IRB treasurer for the south of England.

Michael returned to Ireland to play a part in the Easter Rising of 1916 in Dublin. British forces captured him and interned him in Frongoch in North Wales. On his release in 1916, he strengthened his involvement in Sinn Féin. In December 1918 he was elected as a Sinn Féin Member of Parliament of Cork South. He was also present when Dáil Éireann was established in January 1919, which announced an Irish Republic.

Continued British efforts to suppress the Republican movement led to Michael's role as Director for the Irish Republican Army (IRA) in the Irish War of Independence. Despite persistent efforts, the British were unable to capture Michael. A truce was signed in July 1921 and Michael acquiesced to Irish president Eamon de Valera's (1882–1975) request to serve on the peace-making talks headed by Arthur Griffith. The treaty struck on 6 December 1921 involved Dominion status and excluded six counties in Ireland which split Dáil Éireann views. Civil war ensued

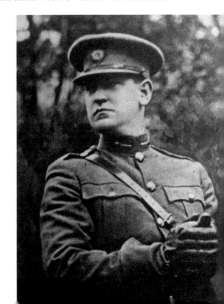

Photograph of Michael Collins. (Cork City Museum)

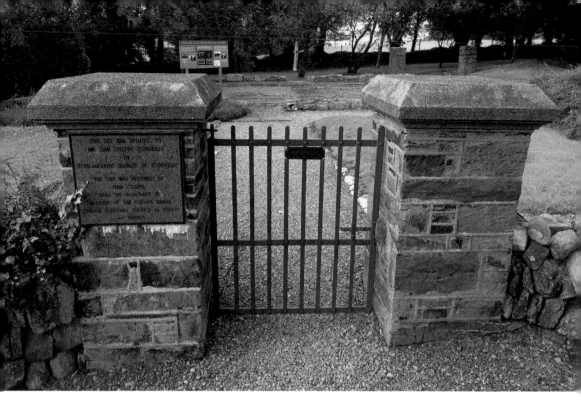

Birthplace of Michael Collins, Sam's Cross, Clonakility.

between the two sides. On 22 August 1922, Michael was assassinated at Béal na mBláth, County Cork.

The first ever commemoration at Béal na mBláth took place twelve months after Michael's death. On 21 June 1923 Richard Mulcahy led Free State troops in erecting a small wooden cross. Floral wreaths were laid, mass was delivered by an army chaplain and Mulcahy gave a short oration. A year later on 23 August 1924 another ceremony led by General Eoin O'Duffy, and chairman of the Free State government, W. T. Cosgrave, unveiled a large limestone one to replace the wooden cross. As the years progressed this minor road on which the memorial stands, complete with platform to accommodate an annual oration to the site of Irish history's most infamous ambush, was slowly widened.

In 1964 a site was acquired at Sam's Cross, Clonakilty, for the erection of a memorial to Michael Collins. A 10-ton granite stone from the Wicklow mountains formed the memorial. A bronze plaque showing a profile of Collins is set into the face of the slab. The plaque was designed by Cork sculptor Mr Seamus Murphy RHA, who had already completed a bust of Michael. It was unveiled on Sunday 18 April 1965 by Tom Barry. Nearby the ruins of the foundations of the Collins' family house can be visited. In October 1990, the Michael Collins Centre just off the Clonakilty–Timoleague road was opened as a visitor centre.

In 2002 the first statue of Michael Collins was unveiled at the edge of Emmet Square in Clonakilty. The project was led by Tim and Dolores Crowley of the Michael Collins Centre and members of Clonakilty Historical Society. The sculptor Kevin Holland was commissioned to create a 7-foot bronze statue. More recently, in 2016 the Michael Collins House opened in Clonakilty, which is a new museum dedicated to the life and times of Michael.

7. A Causeway to a Virgin Gaze – Inchidoney Island

Inchidoney's fine sandy beach is a very popular gem with day trippers from Cork City and the region. Located around 2.5 miles from Clonakilty, at one time Inchidoney was a pure island and could only be accessed by a causeway across a salt marsh and when the tide was out. The two 'coursed dressed rubble' limestone causeways were only developed *c.* 1890. In April 1985 archaeological excavations by Rose Cleary in the heart of the island unearthed six earth-cut chambers, which were deemed to be medieval in date and possibly were part of a ringfort. Nearby was a medieval church, which by the year 1615 was in need of repair and in ruins by 1693.

On the outbreak of the Confederate wars of 1641 between English and Irish families the English settlers in Clonakilty were compelled to fly to Bandon. Almost immediately on the English withdrawal from the town the forces left behind were attacked by multitudes of the native Irish on all sides. A well-contested battle was the result, and the Scottish troops, refusing to retire, were cut to pieces. The Bandon forces on the other hand had resources and succeeded in partly defending themselves in an old fort on the within Rosscarbery wood until reinforcements arrived. Unitedly the combined elements attacked and the Irish forces were forced to take refuge on the strand of Inchidoney Island. The tide swept in and around 700 of them were drowned.

Post-1641 the Hungerford family of Farley in Somerset under Captain Thomas Hungerford settled in west Cork. He bought significant estates in the Rosscarbery area and on 28 October 1674 purchased Rathbarry Castle from Edward Williams. The Hungerfords married into many other influential families in the area including Beecher, Jones and Daunt.

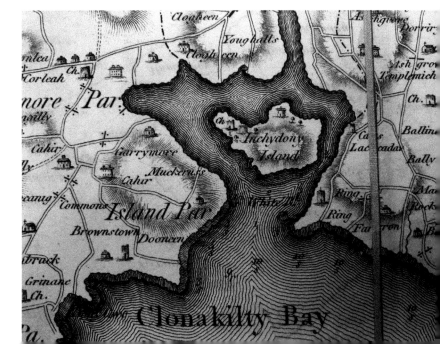

Inchidoney Island, as illustrated in the Grand Jury Map of Cork, 1811. (Cork City Library)

At the time of Griffith's Valuation, Thomas Hungerford was leasing his Inchidoney property from the Ecclesiastical Commissioners when it was valued at £22. In the 1870s both Mary Sandes Hungerford and Francis Hungerford, of the Island House, Inchidoney, were the owners of over 500 acres in County Cork in the 1870s. As time progressed, later heirs of the Hungerford estate emigrated to Canada and Australia, ending the family's connection with the area. Hungerford House is now the site of a retreat centre.

The advent of the nineteenth century coincided with the collection of the folklore of the appearance of the Virgin Mary on the coastal side of the island. Story collector and poet Joseph Callanan in his *c.* 1820 works recounts a local story of the Virgin Mary standing on an elevated sand bank. According to folklore, she was discovered kneeling there by the crew of a vessel that was coming to anchor near the place. They laughed at and insulted her, upon which a storm arose and destroyed the ship and her crew. Attached to the story is the local shell narrative or the 'Virgin Mary' shell story, as it is called. They are the grey, fragile shell of the sea potato, a spined urchin-like creature that burrows in the sand. It is still recounted in the area today that the 'M' shape of tiny perforations on the upper surface are said to symbolise Mary, the Mother of God. The dots reflect the number the beads of the Rosary, and, on the reverse side, some see the Sacred Heart.

In the twentieth century, the promotion of areas such as Inchidoney Island to increase tourism was driven by the Irish Free State's Irish Tourist Association (ITA), which was established in 1925 to market the young Irish Free State as a tourist destination internationally. Small resorts along the Cork coastline were developed simultaneously at sites such Garryvoe, Ballycotton, Kinsale, Courtmacsherry, Glandore, Bantry Bay, Glengarriff and Berehaven.

In the early 1930s Inchidoney Ocean Hotel, as it was originally called, was opened. Newspapers from the time detail that the resort, on 150 acres, boasted quality hard tennis courts and a nine-hole golf links. Bathing, boating and fishing were among the other activities enjoyed by the hotel's residents. Equipped with a ballroom, dances and fancy-dress parties were regularly held at the hotel. Inchidoney Island Lodge & Spa stands on the site of the former hotel, which was demolished in 1997.

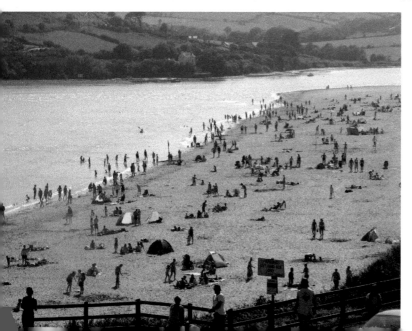

Inchidoney Beach.

8. An Estate and Its Countryfile – Castlefreke Estate

The former estate of Castlefreke is peaceful as one treks through the An Coilte forestry tracks and discovers its historic fabric. The year 1641 marked a change of the guard at Rathbarry Castle. During the Confederate wars, the fifteenth-century castle of Randal Óg Barry was besieged by Irish forces and fell. A year later the castle was purchased by Arthur Freke.

Arthur's great-grandfather was Robert Freke, who was auditor of the treasury in the reigns of Henry VIII and Elizabeth I. Robert's estate was worth upwards of £100,000 on his death. He had eight children. His son and heir was Sir Thomas Freke, who was born 27 September 1563 and knighted by James I. William was the son of Thomas. Born in 1577, William married Ann, daughter of Arthur Swaine of Sareen in Hampshire. William and Ann had twelve children in the midst of which they moved to Ireland. Their son Arthur was born in Hampshire, England, in 1604. Arthur married Dorothy Smith, daughter of Sir Piercy Smith Knight (Percy Smyth) of Youghal.

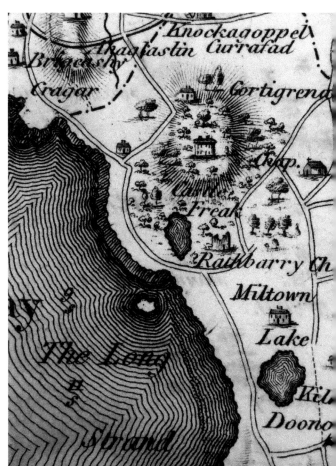

Castle Freke, as illustrated in the Grand Jury Map of Cork, 1811. (Cork City Library)

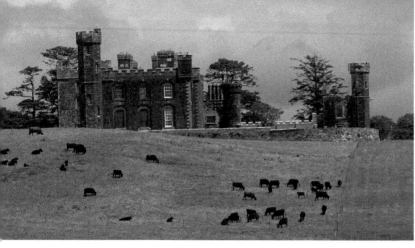

Reparing the walls of Castlefreke Castle.

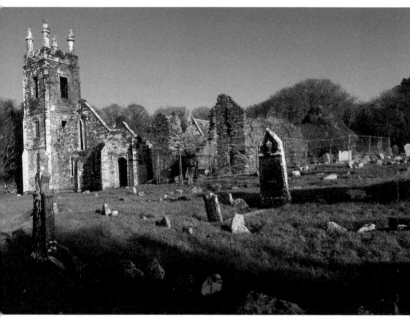

Ruin of Church of Ireland, Castlefreke.

Very little of the old castle site has survived within nineteenth-century farm buildings on the site – a coachyard, rounded arch, two noticeably thick walls, a tall revetment wall built against a rock face and a locked-up semicircular arched opening for a cannon. During the eighteenth century a mansion was constructed nearby. This was added to in 1807 with Gothic Revival features, comprising bartizans, towers, castellations and tall chimneystacks. The courtyard was remodelled and a second courtyard created with the addition of a single-storey wing and tower. This work took several decades to complete. In 1910 fire destroyed the interior and architects Kaye-Parry and Ross introduced concrete floors, a roof and a Jacobean Revival-style interior. In 1919 the last Baron of Carbery, John Evans-Freke, sold the estate.

The lands were divided when it passed to the Land Commission in the 1930s. It was used as army barracks for the 38th and 39th Battalions during the Second World War, and later as a summer base for the boys of Upton Industrial School. The house was dismantled in 1952 following the purchase of the house by a local man. It has undergone several refurbishment projects over the past few decades.

Many estate features survive from the impressive and scenic demesne of Castle Freke. The demesne enclosing wall is impressive and dates to *c.* 1840. It comprises vertically aligned rubble stone fabric, which run uninterrupted for many kilometres. The remains of a walled garden exist to the north-east with an octagonal tower in the woods surviving to the north-west.

Within the demesne lie two ruinous Church of Ireland churches, which were built by the Freke family. The earliest ruined church was in need repair in 1615 but was ruins by 1693. The interior contains numerous headstones including the tomb of Ralph Freke, who died in 1717. In 1825, the second church was built just a few metres away. Investment in its architectural design and detailing make it stand out from other churches constructed in the county in the early part of the nineteenth century. It is now roofless, though the ruinous walls stand at full height. The church was closed in 1927.

Other large structures comprise gate lodges (*c.* 1820), a rectory (1820), estate workhouses (1820), a parish hall (1825), a Roman Catholic church (1832) and a sprigging school. The latter school was developed in 1825 by Lady Carbery to link in with the local market for handmade lace. The term 'sprigging' derives comes from the type of lace connected with Rathbarry, which was known as sprigging lace as it was shaped like a sprig or spray.

On high ground in the south of the former estate is an imitation high cross, which is 30 feet high – the largest memorial cross in Ireland. It was erected in 1901 in memory of the 9th Baron of Carbery, who died in 1898.

9. Protecting the Coast – Galley Head Lighthouse

On all approaches, the lighthouse at Galley Head is a significant landmark that can be viewed from both land and sea. From Long Strand for example, it is photogenic, giving extra weight to the scenery of the adjacent cliffs. Immediately adjacent to the lighthouse is the ruined Duneady Castle, which once belonged to the Barry family – a marker that the lighthouse is not the first lookout on the site.

The first proposals for a lighthouse came in the mid-nineteenth century when multiple news stories of wrecked vessels off this jagged coast – in 1846 and 1857 – provoked local MPs and Lord Bandon to act. They lobbied the Board of Trade, and continued political pressure led to correspondence by the board to Admiral Forbes, Commander-in-Chief of the British Navy stationed at Queenstown (now Cobh). Further to this an inspection took place, with a report issuing in March 1871. The project was sanctioned in April 1871. Land on Galley Head and a lease was negotiated over two years by Commissioners of Irish Lights (est. 1786).

The lighthouse was designed by Mr John Swan Sloane, Engineer-in-Chief of the Commissioners of Irish Lights. Mr Sloane had thirty years of experience as a surveyor and architect. During this time, he was involved in lighthouse engineering – drawing

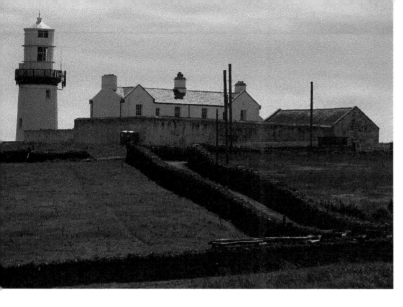

Galley Head
Lighthouse.

up George Halpin's plans for Fastnet Lighthouse. He was superintendent of works for the Commissioner of Irish Lights, procuring lenses abroad in Paris and publishing a Manual for Lightkeepers in 1873. His important piece of work was Galley Head Lighthouse. The contract for the tower was completed by William M. Murphy and his firm from Bantry. It took two years to build. It was to be complemented by light keepers' houses. Messrs J. Edmundson & Co. of Dublin, with their engineer John R. Wigham, supplied the gas-making plant, lantern and French manufactured 'first order dioptric quadriform optic'.

On 21 September 1877, the Commissioners of Irish Lights gave notice that on and after 1 January 1878, a Group Flashing Light would be exhibited at Galley Head between sunset and sunrise: 'The focal plane is 17 ½ feet above the sea, and the Light will be visible, in clear weather, from the sea, between the bearings of East (Northerly) and West by North (Westerly), at a distance of nineteen nautical miles. This light will exhibit a group of six or seven Flashes, in quick succession, every minute'. Such was the impressiveness of the light. Around 1895 Galley Head became a tourist point off the Cork Bandon and South Coast Railway.

In 1907 use of quadriform gas was converted to incandescent paraffin. Later, in 1969, a further conversion took place to electric power. Manual operation continued

Galley Head.

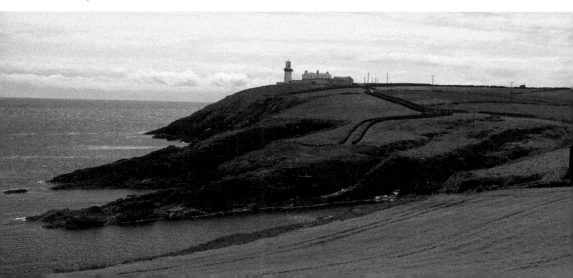

until 1979 when automatic operation was introduced. The principal lighthouse keeper then became an attendant.

The need for the attendant to live at the station was discontinued from 1 July 1997 and changes were made to the station to allow this. The remote control and monitoring room at Dun Laoghaire replaced an onsite presence. A year later two of the old keepers' dwellings were leased to the Irish Landmark Trust. They were restored and are now let to the general public as holiday homes. They are two of twelve All-Ireland lighthouses you can now stay in.

10. A Compass in the Landscape – Drombeg Stone Circle

Drombeg is one of Ireland's most famous stone circles and is also part of a suite of circles and standing stones in West Cork. It is also one of the most publicly accessible. On the winter solstice on 21 December each year, the sun sets over the recumbent stone on the stone circle. If you stand looking between the two portal stones, you will view the sun set in a notch in the opposite hill and over the recumbent stone, which is diametrically across from the two portal stones.

Drombeg was one of the earliest ancient sites protected by the National Monuments Act, 1930. It was added to the list of protected structures by the state in 1938. However, a glance through the Archaeological Inventory of West Cork reveals a myriad of ancient standing stones, stone circles and fulacht fia (ancient cooking sites) – all very much present in the heritage DNA of the region.

Drombeg Stone Circle, Winter Solstice, 2018.

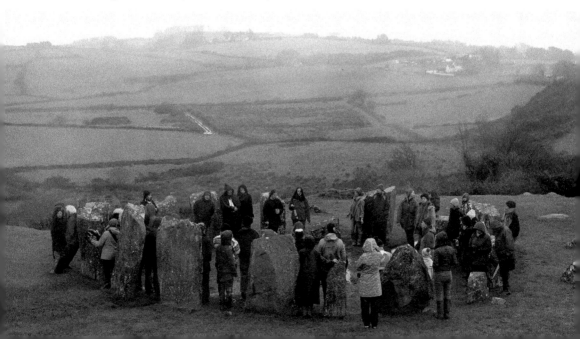

The Drombeg Stone Circle complex is located on a natural rock terrace on the southern slope of a low hill. The circle was excavated 1957 and the nearby fulacht fiadh and hut site was excavated in 1958. The circle comprises seventeen stones – two missing and one fallen. Five pits were uncovered within the circle, sealed beneath compacted gravel floor. One pit contained a cremated human bone, fragments of shale and numerous shards of coarse fabric pots. Other finds from the circle included seven pieces of flint and a small convex scraper.

The excavator of the site, archaeologist Edward Fahy, literally put Drombeg on the map as the findings drew much media attention and were published in the eminent *Journal of the Cork Historical and Archaeological Society*. It was one of Edward's first excavations. Up to then he had been a student at the Cork School of Art. He worked with Michael J. O'Kelly, the curator of Cork Public Museum in Fitzgerald's Park, especially in designing the cases for display when the museum officially opened on 4 April 1945. The building up of the museum's collections and displays was a continuing effort and while engaged in that work, he studied for and was awarded with distinction the Diploma of the Museums Association. This required the writing of a dissertation coupled with specialised courses and examinations in England.

Subsequently Edward Fahy pursued a BA degree, which he obtained with first class honours in archaeology and geography. He took part in many of Michael J. O'Kelly's excavations at this time and built up his experience in fieldwork and excavation techniques. Following his BA, he began work on a Master's degree in archaeology, and for his thesis he undertook the excavation of all the sites in the Lee Valley, which were to disappear because of the ESB's hydro-electric scheme.

11. Etched in Legend – Leap and Its Myths

Leap is a clear reminder that folklore is also a gem embedded in the historical consciousness of West Cork. In 1937–38, with the help of the Department of Education, a collection of folklore was initiated throughout the National Schools of the twenty-six counties in an effort to consolidate information on Irish folklore and ultimately a celebration of folklore and identity itself. Teachers and children alike were asked to approach their traditions as if 'it is the first time and perhaps the last time they will be recorded'. Children were encouraged to speak to the oldest living member of their family and their community.

The work was supervised by teachers, written up in copybooks and submitted to the Folklore Commission. The net result was that 4,574 official notebooks were returned to the Commission. This fascinating archive is now in the custody of the Department of Irish Folklore at UCD, and a microfilm copy of the County Cork material has been available for consultation at the Reference Department in Cork County Library for several years. The collection is known as the Schools' Manuscripts Folklore Collection.

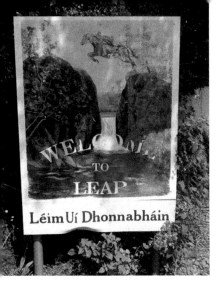

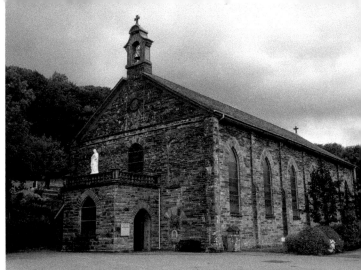

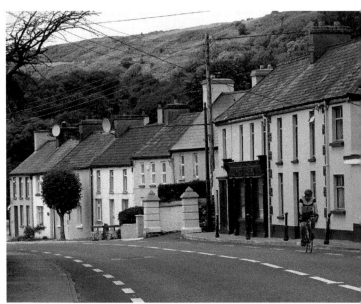

Above left: Welcome to Leap sign illustrating the leap of the priest.

Above right: St Mary's Roman Catholic Church, Leap.

Right: Part of Leap village.

One of origin stories of the place name Leap benefits from that collected by two students. Mary O'Sullivan collected one story from an older person whose name is not recorded. It relates to the time of the Irish Penal Laws:

In the Penal Times mass was said on the side of Cnoc Buide in west Cork. On one occasion, while mass was going on, the call came that the soldiers were coming. The priest took the Blessed Sacrament and leaped on his horse at once and ran. He found the soldiers were closing in on him, and he faced his horse towards a big cliff on the Leap road. The priest thought that he would be killed and he said that if the soldiers were to take the Blessed Sacrament they would take it over his own dead body. But to his surprise instead of falling down the cliff, the horse went through the air, like a bird, and landed on a stone at Newtown about half a mile outside the town of Bantry. That stone is there on the side of the public road still, and nobody dared to touch it.

As context to the story of a priest on the run, the Penal Laws (1691–1829) led to the Banishment Act of 1697 when over 400 Irish secular and regular clerics were expelled to European destinations. Of the regulars who remained in Ireland after the Banishment Act, some found refuge in wealthy Roman Catholic houses while others were able to pass themselves off as secular clergy and to register as such under the act of 1704 for registering Roman Catholic clergy. Many more went to remote destinations to set up makeshift churches such as non-roofed churches and mass rocks.

Pilgrim mass rocks and altars were rooted in poor barren land, bog and rock – border lands of sorts in out of the way locations. Some sites were more temporal and less permanent than others but all were counter monuments to the Penal Laws. Secret sacred sites emerged to host Roman Catholic ceremonies, which were deemed not safe, away from fear of arrest by British soldiers. To gain access to the Catholic religion, it became more pilgrimage orientated. Up to seventy holy wells are recorded in West Cork as well as myriad of mass rocks and the larger pilgrimage complex of cells at Gougane Barra.

12. The Harbour of the Oaks – Glandore Pier

A few kilometres west from Drombeg Stone Circle, the road encounters the beautiful curving pier of Glandore or Cluain Duar in Irish, the 'Harbour of the Oaks'.

The Freeman newspaper of Saturday 28 June 1879 (p. 12) reveals some of its history while announcing the death of Glandore's investor and champion, James Redmond Barry. He had died on the previous Wednesday 25 June 1879 at his residence at Glandore House. He was ninety years old and had at one time been a most prominent figure in the politics of the south of Ireland. He was the head of a very ancient Catholic family. He was one of the most trusted companions of Daniel O'Connell, champion of Catholic emancipation. In the anti-tithe battles

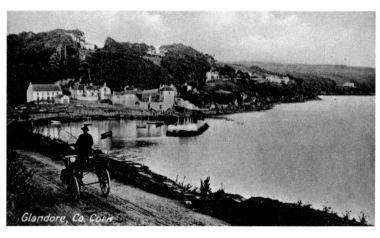

Glandore, Co. Cork

Postcard of Glandore Harbour, *c.* 1910. (Cork City Museum)

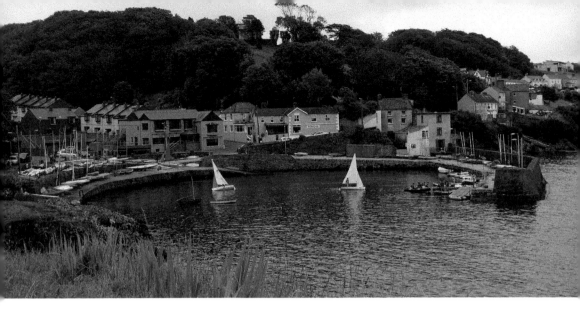

Glandore Pier.

across County Cork James also played a great part, and the government of the day withdrew his honour of being a commissioner of the peace (to which a subsequent government restored him).

With great effort James promoted the local development of education, the fisheries, the mines and the manufactures of the region. He was also one of the first great patrons of popular education in Ireland, and provided funding for a national school, which still stands but has expanded through the years. Samuel Lewis in his *Topographical Dictionary of Ireland* in 1837 remarks of a large school population:

> A school-house capable of containing 600 children, has been lately erected by Mr Barry, with the aid of the National Board of Education the boys receive instruction in agriculture and trades from competent teachers, and a model farm and carpenters' workshop are connected with it.

Around 1820 James Redmond Barry personally spent a sum of over £10,000 upon the development of the village and harbour of Glandore. In 1837 Samuel Lewis remarked that the pier could host twenty fishing boats at any one time:

> A pier has been recently constructed near the village, which affords protection to about 20 fishing yawls of three tons each; fish of every kind is abundant in the bay. Many elegant houses and a comfortable hotel have been erected, and because of the beauty of its situation and the salubrity of the climate, the village has become a favourite place of residence, and much frequented during the bathing season.

As an MP James Redmond Barry promoted the need for Westminster to invest in fishermen and protect their interests in every way. In the 1850s he was appointed a Commissioner of Irish Fisheries. He campaigned for navigation markings off Glandore Harbour and for a boatyard in the nearby Union Hall. In 1870 James Redmond Barry was a prominent landlord, owning over 400 acres in County Cork. He also promoted agricultural methods training for his tenants by providing a model farm school in the local area.

13. The Hook of a Story – Union Hall

The further you delve into the countryside of West Cork the more you are attracted into other historic corners. Poulgorm Bridge is a ten-span concrete bridge over Glandore Harbour, which was built *c.* 1890. It connects the village of Glandore to Union Hall village.

An anchor on display at the outskirts of the village is dated from the early eighteenth century and once belonged to a French ship, whose name is now lost to time. It is deemed to be the largest one of that era to be recovered from Irish waters. While lying on the seabed, Locals were not aware that a massive anchor lay on the seabed and so it caused much annoyance to the local fishermen who caught their nets on it. The feature was known as the hook. In May 1999, the anchor was discovered accidently by the FV *Ros Anee*, when its nets got caught on its tip. A team of divers on board the MV *Neachtain* raised it from the seabed. They donated it to the people of Myross as a symbol representing the close connection of the area to the sea.

Historical panels in Union Hall record that the Irish name for the area was Bean Traigh, which dated back to ancient times. It means 'foul-smelling strand' and was believed to be derived from warriors killed in battle on or near the Clontaff townland or Cluain an Chatha, meaning 'plain of the battle'. The bodies from the battle were placed on the strand for the tide to carry away. Another old Irish name for Union Hall is Traigh an Bhroin, 'strand of lamentation'.

The Union Hall derivation is said to have got its name from a hall built to commemorate the passing into law of the Act of Union of Great Britain and Ireland in 1801.

The advent of the nineteenth century brought a change in political circumstances for Ireland. The fear of further rebellions in Ireland and of renewed foreign support caused the passing of the Act of Union. This act abolished the separate Irish Parliament. From then/1801 until 1922, Ireland was to be governed directly from London.

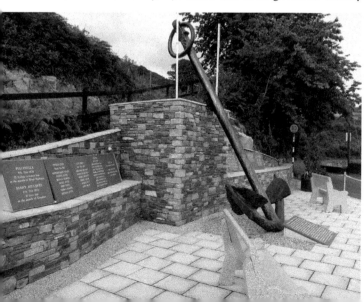

Early eighteenth-century anchor from a French ship.

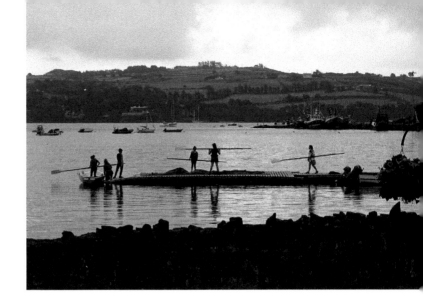

Union Hall.

14. The Roots of the Past – Castletownsend and Its Curiosities

Castletownsend lies deep in the heart of the West Cork coastline and possesses a number of curiosities to explore. Anciently, Castletownsend had the name Glanbarrahane, derived from a deep rocky glen dedicated to St Barrahane, a local fifth-century hermit saint.

Richard Townsend, an officer in the Cromwellian army, acquired Castle Townsend and other lands in West Cork in the late 1660s (6,543 acres). He quickly fortified his harbour holdings. On top of a steep incline on the south shore of Castle Haven bay, he constructed a small star-shaped fort, which became known as Bryan's Fort. Now quite overgrown and in a ruinous state, the visitor can still explore part of it. In 1690 the fort and the garrison came under attack by the O'Driscoll family, who had pledged their allegiance to the cause of James II. Around 500 Irish soldiers besieged the garrison. In the first wave of attacks, Fineen O'Driscoll lost forty men, a commander and two officers but rallied again to take the garrison a second time.

The original Townsend castle was built and is still occupied by the Townsend family. Several phases of construction can be viewed with the central two-storey block forming its historic core. A two-storey porch dates to the original occupation around 1650. The towers were added later, using stones from the ruins of an earlier castle. A single-bay three-storey crenulated tower to the north-east was added around 1860.

The village developed around the castle. A unique feature of it are the two sycamore trees growing in the roundabout in the centre of the village. The present sycamores replace two trees planted in the 1800s. In 1837, Samuel Lewis in

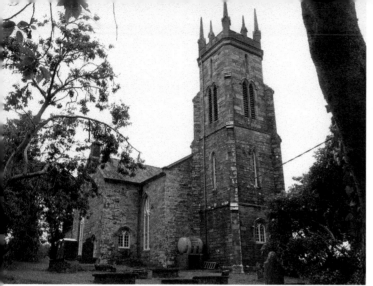
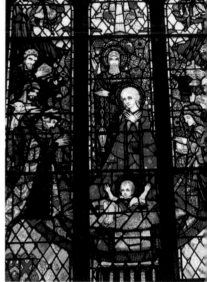

Above left: St Barrahane's Church of Ireland, Castletownsend.

Above right: The Nativity with the Adoration of the Kings and the Shepherds, with Saints Brigid, Fachtna and Barr, St Barrahane's Church of Ireland, Castletownsend.

his *Topographical Dictionary of Ireland* details life across the one main street and the shorter one diverging from it.

> The village comprised 150 houses, which are mostly small but well built. It contains the custom house for the port of Baltimore and is a coast-guard station in the district of Skibbereen, and a constabulary police station ... The Harbour, which is half a mile wide, is well sheltered, and vessels of 500 tons' burden can anchor within the haven.

St Barrahane's Church of Ireland is also set on higher grounds within the former estate with fifty-two steps to the top – a step for each Sunday of the year. It sits atop the site of an earlier church built in 1761. The current church was designed by well-respected architect James Pain, who used stone from Horse Island. The Board of First Fruits, a body tasked with promoting the Protestant religion in Irish regions, granted £1,250. Colonel Townsend gave £250. Inside the timber panelling and organ gallery is impressive, as is the mosaic and Harry Clarke-designed stained-glass windows.

Henry Patrick (Harry) Clarke, Ireland's most renowned stained-glass artist, was born in Dublin in 1889. Some of Harry's most celebrated work includes the nine windows he created for the Honan Chapel at Cork University; The Eve of St Agnes at the Hugh Lane Municipal Gallery of Modern Art in Dublin; the Life of Christ windows at Díseart in Dingle; the set of decorative windows at Bewley's cafe, Dublin; and the Geneva window, now at the Wolfsonian in Miama, Florida. Harry's book illustrations continue to fascinate and delight readers worldwide as his illustrations are highly sought after.

In St Barrahane's Church there is the three-light window entitled the Nativity with the Adoration of the Kings and the Shepherds, with saints Brigid, Fachtna and Barrahane (1918); the two other windows are saints Louis IX, King of France, and Martin of Tours (1921), and the exquisite lancet, Saint Luke attended by saints Cecelia, Barrahane and Fidelio (1926).

15. The Mournful Countryside – Skibbereen and the Great Famine

After leaving Clonakilty, each step that we took westward brought fresh evidence of the truth of the reports of the misery, as we either met a funeral or a coffin at every hundred yards, until we approached the country of the Shepperton Lakes. Here, the distress became more striking, from the decrease of numbers at the funerals, none having more than eight or ten attendants, and many only two or three (Eyewitness report on the great hunger by James Mahoney, *Illustrated London News*, 1847).

There is consensus among historiographers, both Irish and international, that the West Cork region suffered inordinately in the years of the Great Famine, 1845–50, and the Skibbereen area has become synonymous with it worldwide. Between 1841 and 1851 the population of Ireland fell by around twenty per cent. In fact, during the famine years (1845–50) the population declined by around 2.5 million. Emigration counted for some 1.5 million of this.

While one cannot say that the Great Famine story is a gem, the passing down of the deep respect for the effects of the Great Famine and collective memory of it pervades the identity of those raised in West Cork. It is this deep respect that is a gem of great note. The memorials adjacent to the Famine Pits at Abbeystrowry, it is recorded that between 8,000 and 10,000 famine victims are buried at this site. There

Below left: Skibbereen Heritage Centre.

Below right: Famine victim in Clonakilty begging for alms to bury her dead child, 1847, from the *Illustrated London News*, Cork. (Cork City Library)

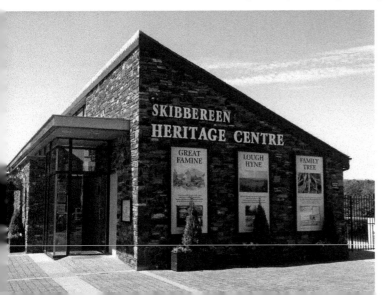

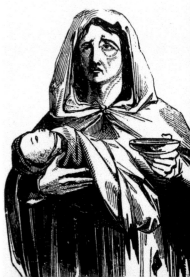

were two other burial grounds in operation also, and many hundreds were buried in ditches or gardens.

The Skibbereen Union area was one of the most severely stricken regions in the country. Truth be told it is impossible to say how many people died in the Skibbereen Union area during those years. Certainly, the evocative pictures that appeared in the *Illustrated London News* depict a population just surviving in fourth-class mud cabins, images of eviction, images of harsh poverty and haunting images of death.

Over many decades, the Skibbereen Trail has been developed and leads the walker to sites that have direct links with the Great Irish Famine. Each site is unique. Some commemorate great works of philanthropy, others of emigration, more of relief schemes, while others tell of famine, fever and death.

One story relates that on Wednesday 30 September 1846 between 800 and 1,000 roadworkers arrived in Skibbereen. They were given back-breaking jobs on the Public Works Relief Scheme north of the town. Wages were low, around 8*d* a day, and often workers had to wait weeks for their money. Another story relates to Skibbereen Union Workhouse and Fever Hospital, which was designed to ensure that only the really destitute would seek admission. The workhouse was built to accommodate 800 people, but at the height of the famine it was grossly overcrowded. Many unclaimed victims from the workhouse were buried in an adjoining paupers' graveyard.

During the 1990s, 150 years after the Great Famine, reflections on some of the sites above and similar ones emerged and a major refurbishment was carried out on the local graveyard by the local community. Skibbereen Heritage Centre opened in 2000 and aimed to support a resurgence in interest following the anniversaries across the countryside. The centre is a focal point for those interested in the Great Famine period. It continues to connect with to second and third generation Irish in England, Australia, the USA and Canada, who may welcome an opportunity to study it in more detail.

16. The Biology of Place – Lough Hyne and a European Marine Reserve

Lough Hyne, around 4 miles south-west of Skibbereen, is a sea lough of acknowledged national and international scientific importance. There is a very wide range of important habitats within the lough and its seaward approaches, a range seldom found in more extensive areas elsewhere.

Marine research work first began there in 1886, making it one of the oldest marine reserves in Europe. Since 1886 some very exceptional scientists have worked there over the decades. Professor Louis Renouf was a hugely influential figure in Lough Hyne's establishment as a 'biological station' in the 1920s and his work attracted some of the major scientists of the era to visit and carry out research. Robert Lloyd

Praeger introduced Renouf to the lake in 1923 and he, in turn, brought people like Sir Julian Huxley to the lake to work. Huxley was a founder member of the World Wildlife Fund, the first director of UNESCO and a great friend of Louis Renouf. Other scientists carried on from Renouf's lead, many of them returning year after year to do so. Jack Kitching first visited the lake from Bristol University in 1938 and continued to carry out research there until 1986 while his colleague John Ebling, who first came to Lough Hyne in 1937, visited until 1976.

Lough Hyne's sheltered position, surrounded by high lands at all sides, means that it's a safe place to dive and carry out research. The rise and fall of the tide is only around 1 metre within the lake compared with 3.5 metres in the sea outside, which also affects its ecology. In addition, as there are no significant fresh water sources draining into the lake, it is truly a marine environment, its salinity equivalent to

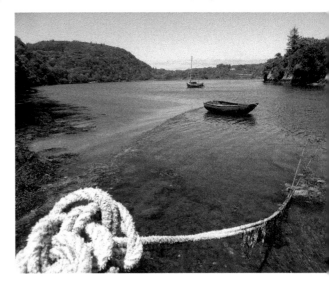

Right and below: Lough Hyne.

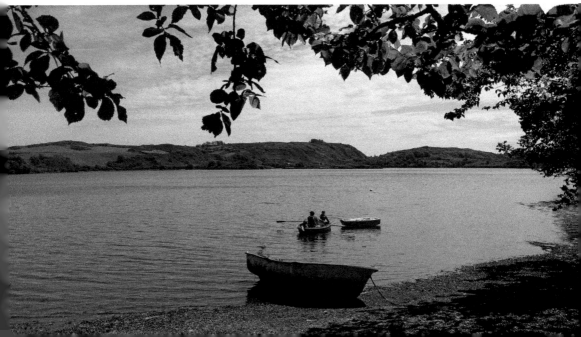

that of the sea outside. These factors, alongside its habitat variety, result in a wide diversity of flora and fauna within the lake, including a number of rare species. While Lough Hyne is less than 1 square kilometre in area, it has diverse marine habitats. Possibly the most exceptional of these is 'the Rapids', the narrow channel of water that connects the lough to the sea and allows tidal interchange between it and the sea outside. In addition, watch the Phytoplankton within Lough Hyne at night as it causes the glow-in-the-dark effect (bioluminescence).

Skibbereen Heritage Centre shows an audio-visual documentary of the unusual tidal species to be found in the lake as well as running through the local legends of the area and the ancient myth of the local king with donkey ears.

17. A Bejewelled Knapsack – Baltimore Castle

All of Baltimore is a gem – its colours, laneways, pier area and in particular its castle. The castle of Dún na Séad (Fort of the Jewels), which gives the village its Irish name, is open to the public. Inside the visitor can read a myriad of information panels about the history of the castle and about the work of Patrick and Bernie McCarthy, who began the work of restoration of an empty ruin in 1997.

The effects of the Anglo-Norman invasion led Henry II to grant to his knights Robert Fitzstephen and Miles de Cogan half the kingdom of Cork. Fitzstephen adopted several Irish customs, even taking the name Lord Sleynie. In 1215 Richard de Carew, a descendent of Robert Fitzstephen, built the castles of Dún na Gall and Dún na Séad in Baltimore. Richard was also the son of an Anglo-Norman and Gaelic marriage – his father being Richard de Carew and his mother whose name was Raghenidla McCarthy, who was a daughter of the Gaelic chieftain King Dermod MacCarthy of Cork.

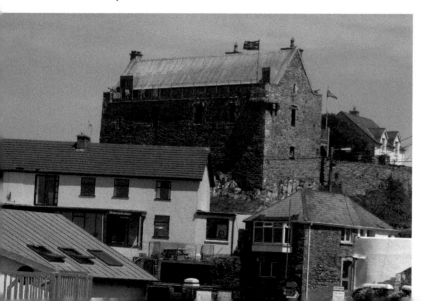

Baltimore Castle.

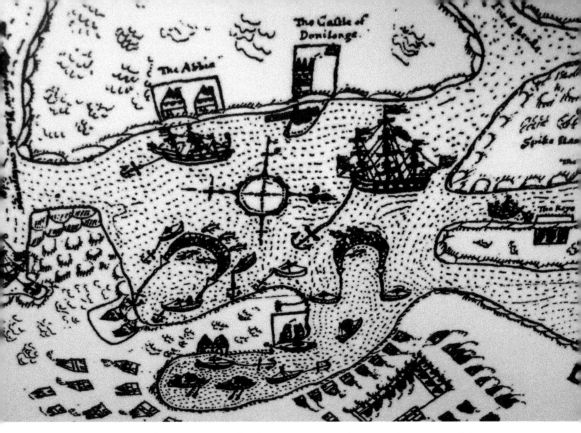

Early seventeenth-century map of Baltimore Castle and bay. (Baltimore Castle)

By the middle of the thirteenth century, Fineen McCarthy became chieftain and he began contesting English control of the territory. Attacking English castles, he slayed many of their occupiers. Soon after, Irish clans began the process of retaking ownership of their lands and the O'Driscoll family took possession of Dún na Séad. Over the next three centuries, the O'Driscoll clan grew considerably in strength and maritime influence along the south-west coast of Ireland. Some of the family members even engaged in piracy.

In 1601, at the Battle of Kinsale, Sir Fineen O'Driscoll allied himself with the Spaniards and handed over Dún na Séad and his lands to the Spanish commander Don Juan del Aguila. At the same time he supplied several English warships with fresh provisions. For this he was later pardoned by Elizabeth I for his part in the Battle of Kinsale. He later leased lands in the area to the new English planter Sir Thomas Crook, who arrived from Cornwall. Thomas first procured a charter of incorporation from James I. The charter was issued on 25 March 1613. He next divided the town into several tenements with lots for gardening. He gave to each inhabitant leases of convenient land for building or grazing.

The English planters are remembered for the fact that in June 1631 two Algerian ships raided Baltimore and captured 107 of them, who were then sold into slavery on the African market. The event is called the Sack of Baltimore. There is no record of their fate as no ransom was paid for them and none ever returned. Extra soldiers were drafted into the area to protect the coastline but many of the planters moved northwards to live in the new plantation towns of Clonakilty and Skibbereen. By the late seventeenth century the castle itself had fallen into disrepair and was a ruin for nearly 300 years.

The view from the top of Baltimore Castle shows the pier area, which was constructed by the Congested Districts Board in 1880. From 1879, Baltimore had developed as a centre of an expanding mackerel fleet. Eleven steamers brought the spring mackerel to England on an almost daily basis. In 1887, the Baltimore Fishing School for the training of 150 boys in a fishing occupation was founded. In 1893, a new spur rail track from Skibbereen to Baltimore was opened to transport the fish to other markets in the city and county.

18. A Coastal Pillar – Baltimore Beacon

Outside Baltimore atop a cliff face is the unique Baltimore Beacon, which offers scenic views over Baltimore Harbour and Sherkin Island. The impressive conical white-painted Baltimore Beacon, sometimes called the 'pillar of salt' or 'Lott's wife', is approximately 50 feet (15.2 metres) high and 15 feet (4.6 metres) in diameter at the base. Towards the end of July 1847, Commander James Wolfe, Royal Navy, informed the Ballast Board that he had recently completed a survey of Baltimore Harbour and noticed the destruction of the warning of rocks beacon on the eastern point of the southern entrance to the harbour. Almost a year passed before, on 6 July 1848, the Board requested the secretary to seek permission from Lord Carbery for a piece of ground, 30 feet in diameter, on which to build a new beacon. *The Cork Examiner* on 16 September 1859 (p. 3) records:

> The bay or harbour of Baltimore, through which the journey lies, is admirable as a station for ships, and is most attractive in its picturesque grandeur. It has almost uniformly deep water in the basin and debouches on the sea through an opening of less than the width of our Harbour's Mouth, formed on the right side by Sherkin island, and on the left by the mainland. On either side rise precipitously stupendous cliffs, the highest of which on the left is crowned by a tall tower or beacon, which may be seen at immense distances seaward.

In recent times, the hosting of an interactive map online was developed to facilitate easy access to the Wreck Inventory of Ireland Database compiled by the department's National Monuments Service. At the base of the Baltimore Beacon's cliff lies a green buoy that marks a reef where a Man O'War Ship, called the HMS *Looe*, was grounded in 1697 (and which in time gave its name to the reef). Built only a year earlier in Plymouth in 1696, the thirty-two-gun or 'demi-batterie' frigate was the flagship of the Irish Coast Fleet assigned to patrolling the waters around Ireland. The ship was one of only thirty-four such ships constructed at the time. Stopping at Baltimore for provisions, on leaving the harbour mouth stormy weather grounded the ship on the reef. The crew managed to escape the sinking vessel and to save much of its tackle and cargo. In 2001 the Underwater Archaeology Unit (UAU) of

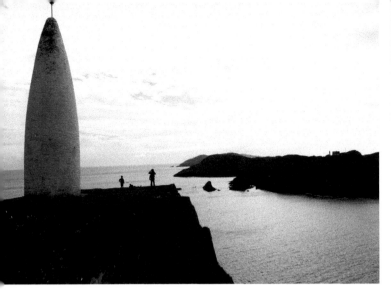
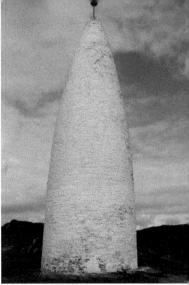

Above left and right: Baltimore Beacon.

the National Monuments Service executed a survey of the wreck site. No structural evidence was found but seven iron guns and numerous cannon balls were discovered at various depths on the reef and the sea floor.

19. Etching a Narrative – Carbery's Hundred Isles

From the Baltimore Beacon the scenery is very picturesque and the visible large and small islands have inspired several writers and poets through the centuries. There is a Latin poem called 'Carberiae Rupes' ('Carbery's Rocks'), which was written by Dean Jonathan Swift, who spent some time in the neighbourhood in 1723. The poem referred to the sea stacks and sea caves common off the West Cork coastline.

The phrase Carbery's Hundred Isles is derived from writer and poet Thomas Davis, who published his poem 'The Sack of Baltimore' in 1844. Thomas was also the instigator of the Young Ireland Nationalist movement, whose work has influenced nationalist narratives of Irish history plus an array of Cork placenames named after him. The poem referenced the raid on the village of Baltimore by Algerian pirates in 1631, in which most of the inhabitants were kidnapped and brought to the slave markets of Algiers. The first line reads: 'The summer sun is falling soft on Carbery's hundred isles'. The poem became popular and the phrase Carbery's One Hundred Isles became engrained in the cultural DNA and tourism promotion literature of the area. However, the number of rocks and islands is just over fifty.

Irish chieftains including the O'Driscolls, the McCarthys, and the O'Mahonys often used their strongholds on these islands to stop the approach of galleys filled with foreign crews, whose tendencies were of a piratical nature. Hence, the Archaeological Inventory for West Cork shows an array of promontory forts across the larger islands.

Religious history is also present. To the west of Hare Island, formerly called Innisdriscoll, are the Keams (islands of St Keam), which are close to the entrance of Whitehall or Rincolisky Bay. There are two islands of this name, the western one being the smaller of the two. Situated upon it were the ruins of an old chapel erected in honour of the memory of St Keam, who is said to have lived in the fifth century. This Keam was a relative of St Kieran, the patron saint of Cape Clear.

The largest islands in the area include Cape Clear and Sherkin Island (both home to several promontory forts, castles and religious historic markers). Other islands also have a rich history, as well as wildlife and a rich biodiversity. They include Calves Island (Calf Island West, Calf Island Middle, Calf Island East), Carthy's Islands (home to large numbers of seabirds, mainly gulls), Castle Island (home of a ruined O'Mahony clan tower house), Catalogues, Sandy, Quarantine and Jeremy Islands, Goat Island (Beg/Mór), Heir Island (home of a cross marking a children's famine memorial), Horse Island (home of copper mines), Inishleigh Island, Long Island (home of Copper Point Lighthouse, built in 1864), Mannin (and Mannin Beg), Rabbit Island, Ringarogy Island, Skeam Islands (west, which has a ruined church from the ninth century AD, and east), and Spanish Island (once home of an O'Driscoll castle).

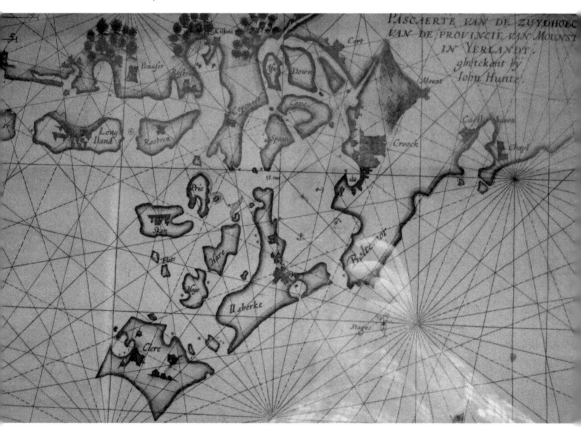

Early seventeenth-century anti-pirate map of Carbery's Isles drawn by Dutch merchant boats. (Baltimore Castle)

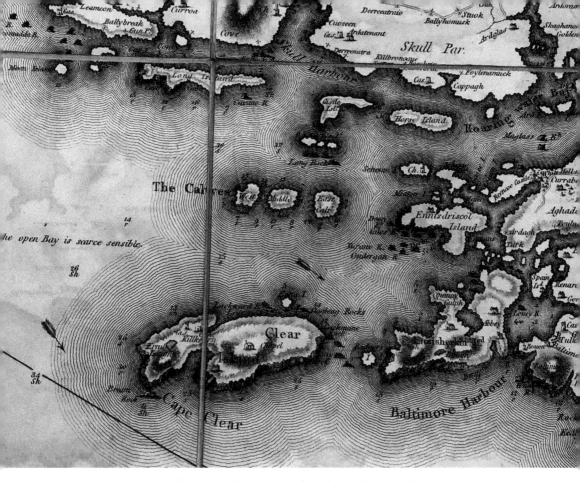

Carbery Isles, 1811, from Grand Jury Map of Cork. (Cork City Library)

20. An International Hub – Sherkin Island Friary

Close to the shore on the eastern side of Sherkin Island is a Franciscan priory founded by Fineen O'Driscoll in 1449. The O'Driscolls lived in a nearby tower house built on a promontory on a cliff face. The ruins of the friary consist of a church with domestic buildings around a cloister to the north. The church consists of a chancel divided by an inserted tower. There is a transept to the south with two side chapels and separating it from the nave is an arcade of three-pointed arches on square piers. The domestic buildings show many alterations and additions. There are also many burials on the ground level of the priory. Adjacent to the friary to the east is the remains of a fish palace. In the seventeenth and eighteenth centuries AD there was also a major pilchard-curing industry based at the former friary in Sherkin and that would have brought in traders as well. There was a huge fishing fleet offloading its catch at Sherkin Island.

In November 2018, a chapter within the *Journal of the Cork Historical and Archaeological Society* showcased the results of excavations at the friary. The excavation team was led by archaeologist Ann Lynch, under the auspices of the National Monuments Service. The excavations revealed the layout of the cloister walks, a system of water management, and most significantly a quantity and variety of ceramics from the area around the friary. Dating to the sixteenth and seventeenth centuries, the shards of pottery had origins in Britain, China, the Low Countries, France, Germany, and Iberia. The variety or origin countries highlights the depth of Baltimore Harbour's international connections.

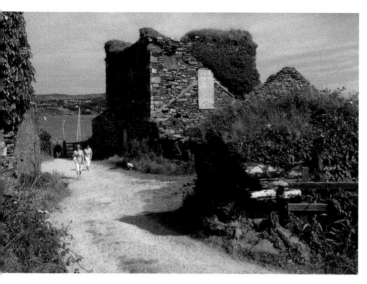

Left: Ruins of Sherkin Island Castle.

Below: Ruins of Sherkin Island Franciscan Friary.

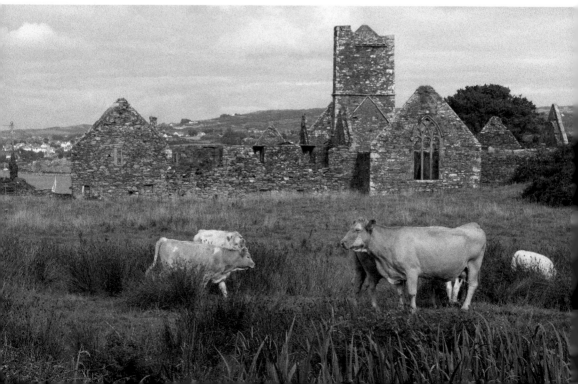

21. Snippets in Time – Cape Clear Museum

Beyond the church ruins and St Ciarán's Well, a pathway extends up Cape Clear Island's steep hills. The community museum lies high up on the ridges of Island. The building was originally a national school for girls but now is filled with local history snippets, folklore, old pictures and artefacts from earlier decades. Information inside the buildings relates that the old school building was abandoned in 1897 when a new schoolhouse was constructed elsewhere near the South Harbour.

In 1970 work commenced on the restoration of the old school building under the direction of an tÁth, Tomás Ó Murchú, the island curate at that time. With the help of Na Campaí Oibre (the work-camp movement) and islanders, the old ruin was, for the most part, rebuilt and reroofed. Groups of voluntary workers from Cork and elsewhere continued to help with the restoration. Roinn na Gaeltachta and AnCo/ FÁS provided funding and training.

In 1979, the building was first used as a museum and exhibition centre under the direction of Éamon Lankford. In 1981, a museum society, Cumann Iarsmalann Chléire, was formed to source, collect and exhibit artefacts of island interest and develop an archive that would comprehensively detail the history, culture and heritage of the island. The centre is open daily during the months of June, July and August and can be visited at other times (winter/spring) by arrangement with the Information Bureau at Trá Chiaráin.

The Heritage Centre includes a museum, exhibition area and archive. Many artefacts of maritime, folk and farm life are exhibited and extensive material has been assembled for inclusion in the museum archive resource. Artefacts include Quern Stone, Saddle Quern and agricultural implements and a copy of the Cape Clear Stone. There is an exhibition on the sailing voyages of Conor O'Brien and Cape Clear Islanders Con and Denis Cadogan in the Baltimore Fishery School-built *Saoirse* (1923) and *Ilen* (1925) boats. Implements used by island and Baltimore shipwrights are on display.

The Fastnet Lighthouse and Fastnet Race Display at the island museum is a twenty-minute audio-visual presentation with mounted exhibition panels recording

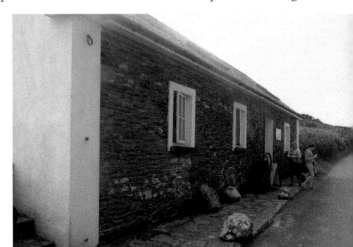

Community Museum, Cape Clear Island.

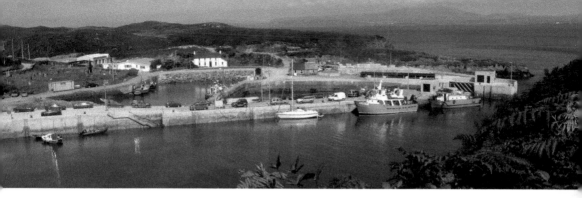

North Harbour of Cape Clear Island.

other aspects of the building of the lighthouses on Cape Clear and the Fastnet Rock. The accompanying exhibition on the biennial Flagship Fastnet Race event pays particular attention to the daring rescue operation conducted by the Rescue Service of the RNLI, Coastguard, RAF and Irish Naval service during the tragic 1979 Fastnet Race. It also has the dramatic rescue off Cape Clear and the Fastnet Rock of the crew of the USA-owned Rambler 100 yacht during the 2011 Fastnet Race.

22. The Teardrop of Ireland – Fastnet Rock

4.5 miles south of Cape Clear is the world-famous Fastnet Rock with its lighthouse. The visitor can take a ferry around the structure from Baltimore to Schull. Marking the country's most southerly point, this important marine navigational mark is also known as the Teardrop of Ireland, because it was the last part of the country seen by emigrants as they set sail for America in bygone days. It is also a historical marker referred to in many information panels in West Cork.

The Commissioners of Irish Lights are the general Lighthouse Authority for all of Ireland and its adjacent seas and islands. The legal basis for the operations of the Commissioners date back to an act passed by the Irish Parliament sitting in Dublin in 1786. In *Salutem Omnium* is the motto of Irish Lights, which in loose translation means 'For the Safety of All'.

On 15 November 1847, a 1,034-ton American liner, the *Stephen Whitney*, sank off Crookhaven with a loss of over ninety lives. The Commissioners of Irish Lights decided to build a lighthouse on the Fastnet Rock, which was completed in 1854. Made of cast iron and brick, it was supposed to withstand everything the Atlantic could throw at it, but by 1865 the sea had swept away part of the rock on which it was built. A new tower was completed by 1903 at a whopping cost of £84,000 – a magnificent engineering feat topped by a powerful light visible for 19 miles. Granite blocks were shipped in from Cornwall for the project and the foreman in charge of construction, James Cavanagh, sometimes stayed a year at a time at the site, overseeing the construction. Each of the 2,000 granite blocks was dressed and dovetailed before shipment. On arrival the blocks had to be reassembled in the eighty-nine courses, which made up the tower.

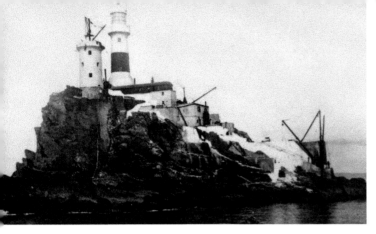

Above: Early twentieth-century construction at Fasnet Rock, 1903. (Cape Clear Museum)

Right: Fastnet Rock.

Around a century ago the wick lamp was in use and burned sperm oil, which had to be liquified by heaters. Colza oil followed and then paraffin. Those old wick lamps were difficult to manage, especially on stormy, winter nights. In the case of colza, for instance, an abundant flow of oil should had to be kept the wick tips, but air in the lantern played an important part in efficient illumination. When seas rose and enveloped the lighthouse dome, ventilation was cut off, and so the light sometimes became extinguished and had to be relit.

The last lighthouse keeper left the Fastnet Rock in April 1993. Before that, three keepers would be on duty at a time, each one watching for four hours then resting for eight.

Nowadays, the Fastnet is famous globally for the Fastnet race (1,126 kms) held every second year. It is a trial of stamina, strength and a battle of wits. First raced for in 1925, seven yachts started the first race and five finished, including the sole Irish entry, Harry Donegan's *Gull*. The race commences from Cowes in the Isle of Wight, battling significant tidal surges. After around 175 nautical miles, the fleet circles Land's End for the lone journey north-west to the Fastnet Rock. There is nothing but ocean waves for another 170 miles until the Fastnet light lifts above the horizon. Rounding the rock is a thrilling experience with all hands on deck to trim the sails for the return leg, another 170 miles to the Bishop Rock off the Scilly Isles, and then 90 miles to the finishing line at Plymouth. Over 240 sailors enter every second year.

23. The Roar of History – The Fastnet Trails

Beyond Skibbereen on the main road to Ballydehob, panoramic views open up of Roaringwater Bay. The bay's name is derived from the sound of the surrounding waters, powered by the Atlantic winds and waves crashing against rocks, cliff faces and islands. Here a package of eight scenic walks across 80 kms of peninsulas and

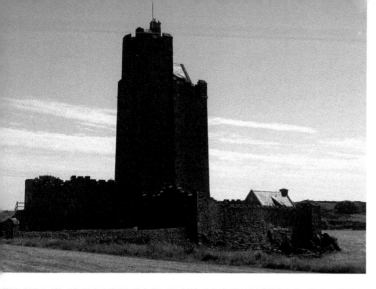

Kilcoe Castle.

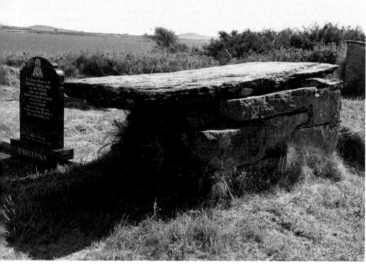

Nineteenth-century
gravestone in Kilcoe
graveyard.

bays can be engaged with. Known as the Fastnet Trails, they crisscross rural roads and were developed in recent years between community councils of Aughadown, Ballydehob and Schull. The area is rich in archaeological sites including Boulder Burials, ringforts, hilltops cairns and stone rows. The area also has a number of old churches and burial grounds, numerous cillíní (children's burial grounds), old piers, old butter roads bound for Cork, and nineteenth-century Roman Catholic and Church of Ireland churches.

There are two castles of interest: Rincoliskey Castle, a home of the O'Driscolls; and Kilcoe Castle, built by the McCarthy family. The view from Kilcoe Castle is exceptional. It overlooks Carbery's Hundred Isles and Roaringwater Bay. Dating back to the mid-1400s, it consists mainly of two towers, which stand corner to corner. The north tower – the highest of the two – contains several rooms connected by staircases. The castle has a very unusual feature in that it does not have a dungeon underground, as would be expected, but on the second floor.

At one time the castle could only be reached by boat or when the tide was low, but there is now a little bridge providing access to the historic site. It also has a very

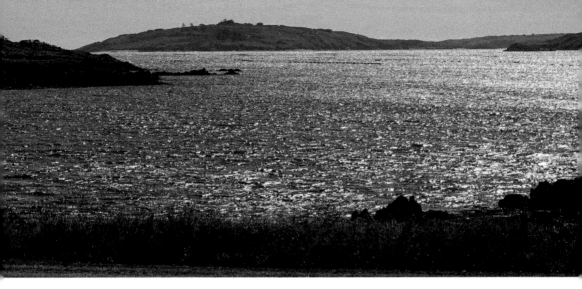

Roaringwater Bay.

proud history and it has the distinction of being the last castle to fall to the English in 1601. After the Battle of Kinsale and the Siege of Dunboy in 1601, the castle was captured by Captain George Flower. Legend has it that after seizing the tower, Captain Flower took the defenders to the top of the castle and executed them. In 1998, the castle was a ruined shell with three vaulted ceilings. The castle was bought by actor Jeremy Irons and restored.

24. Engineering a Future – Ballydehob Viaduct

The old Ballydehob Viaduct is an engineering gem. First mooted in 1883 after the main railway line from Cork had reached Skibbereen, the plan to run a line to Bantry was very ambitious piece of engineering. The project began in 1884 and was paid for by many West Cork ratepayers. It took two years to complete the line, which had a 3-foot narrow gauge and covered a distance of 14.25 miles. The all-in cost was £57,000. The contractors were Messrs McEone and Avigdor, London.

The entire line was quite level but there were a few steep gradients for short lengths and several sharp curves. The only major engineering work is Ballydehob twelve-arched stone viaduct where the track is carried across an inlet of Roaringwater Bay. Ballydehob is the only crossing place, and the other stops were never anything more than roadside halts, although there is a siding at Kilcoe.

Although work on building the permanent way began at the Skibbereen end, the official ceremony of turning the first sod was performed at Ballydehob by the local curate Fr Bernard, who blessed the undertaking. As workmen laid the first sleepers from Skibbereen station the erection of the large, twelve-arched bridge over the sea inlet at Ballydehob was also taken in hand.

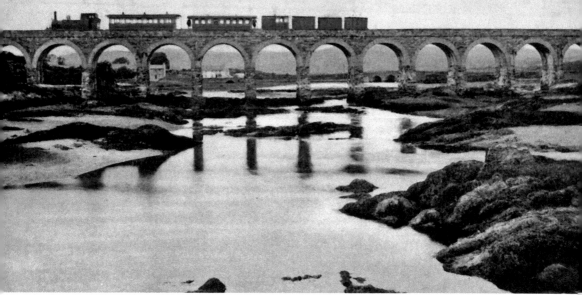

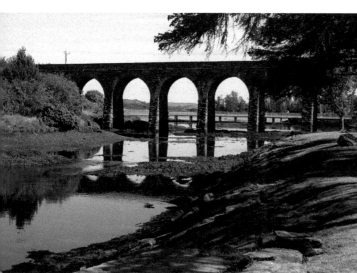

Above: Ballydehob Viaduct, *c.* 1900. (Cork City Museum)

Left: Ballydehob Viaduct. Schull Pier.

Through the years some forty men were steadily employed by this section of the West Cork Railway. The first driver was Augustine Cruise, a native of Cardiff. His fireman was Denny O'Brien of Upper Bridge Street, Skibbereen. The train pulled its way into a then highly industrialised peninsula. Copper mines were being worked at Ballycumisk, Cusheen, Letter and Crookhaven, while barytes deposits at Dreenalomane (near the home of Danno Mahony. world-famed wrestler) were being exploited on a large scale. Besides, the ports of Schull and Crookhaven were being used extensively by fishing and commercial craft. No wonder then that the line had be extended to Schull Pier five years after it was laid.

Perhaps the most distinguished passenger to travel by the 'tram', as the train was called locally, was Guglielmo Marconi. For nearly six years he made his journey by rail and sidecar to and from Brow Head, where he carried out his first experiment in wireless telegraphy.

25. Benchmarks of Maritime Heritage – Schull Pier

There are many scenic and excellently constructed piers in West Cork. At Schull, benches allow the visitor to sit amid nets and fishing boats and appreciate the living maritime heritage. On a ridge overlooking the entrance to the harbour is the location of Scoil Mhuire or Sancta Maria de Scala, a medieval church and school that gave its name to this townland and to Schull Village. As far as can be gathered, the school was run by Finigin O'Mahony, a scholar of renown, who ruled the surrounding country from Rossbrin Castle, situated 3 miles from the town.

The old school overlooked the opening of Schull Harbour into Roaringwater Bay. In the broader coastal region, the seine boat was a narrow fishing boat used off Allihies and Castletownbere area. First introduced in 1622 for pilchard fishing, the same methodology was adapted for mackerel fishing. Each seine comprised two boats, the seine boat and the follower boat or faller as it was called. The seine boat was wider and stronger than the faller as it had to bear greater weight, especially when holding on to the full net of fish. Some of the most seaworthy boats were built in Castletownbere by the Fitzgerald family. The boats were made of hard wood, often larch brought from the woods of Lauragh, and the frames were of oak. Before use the hard wood was sometimes buried in the mud of the strands to harden it further. Nails, which were galvanized if made of copper, were used in the planking only. Oars were made of white deal or very rarely ash.

In 1920 over forty boats of various sizes fished out of Cape Clear, around half of which were motor powered. There were also schooners and yawls. Two hundred people were engaged in full-time fishing on the island. Every Monday or Tuesday morning the adult population would proceed far out to sea – the hookers steering for the inner coastline and the open boats for the neighbourhood of the Fastnet Rock. Sometime in pursuit of their fish, fishermen would go thirty leagues off the land. They remained out during the week and returned on Friday or Saturday with their cargoes

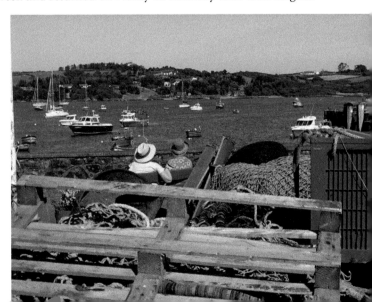

Schull Pier.

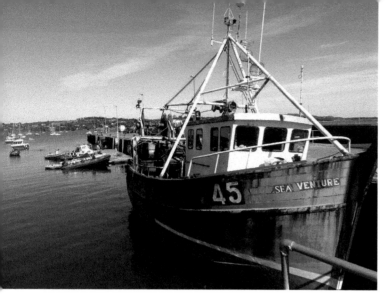

Above and right: Barley

of hake, ling, codfish, congers, and deep-sea fish. The piers around Roaringwater Bay were filled with fish processing plants.

The large extent of fishing from times past has diminished. However, in Schull today there are several nods to rich maritime traditions. Information panels tell the story of the Fastnet Rock lighthouse. There is a modern fish processing plant at the root of the pier where you can buy fresh fish during opening hours. The Schull Rowing Club also has its headquarters on the harbour frontage. Schull Harbour Sailing Club is dynamic with weekend inshore racing throughout the summer season.

The Fastnet International Schools' Regatta happens annually in July, an event for young sailors who contest it from all over Europe. Calves Week takes place in early August annually, the high point of the SHSC racing programme, and this has become a big occasion in the Irish racing programme. It is followed by Schull Harbour Regatta at the weekend with fun for all both ashore and afloat. Ferry trips to Cape Clear Island leave the pier daily throughout the summer. Small boat hire, diving, kayaking and sea angling can all be arranged from businesses within Schull.

26. The Habitats of Landscape – Barley Cove

The ridges about Barley Cove sand dunes appear quickly on narrow roads and bends to reveal the splendour of scenery. As a special area of conservation, the site is particularly important for sand dunes and related habitats that occur at Barley Cove. A fine gradation of habitat occurs from the outer sandy beach through dunes and saltmarshes and then brackish lagoon. Of particular importance is the fixed dune habitat as this is a priority habitat on Annex I of the EU Habitats Directive and is one of the few examples in County Cork and South County Kerry. The dunes merge with a substantial area of saltmarsh that supports both Atlantic and Mediterranean salt meadows.

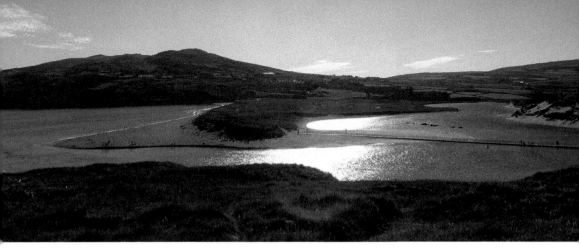

Cove.

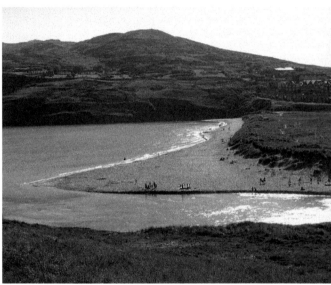

The human story of Barley Cove is also strewn with interesting nuggets on how the sand dunes became an important holiday site in early Irish Free State. On 2 November 1918, a correspondent in the *Skibbereen Eagle* notes that boats of the open yawl nature were net fishing off Barley Cove. One boat with four nets had the remarkable catch of 40,000 beautiful large herrings one night. For the week's fishing these boats had 100,000 herrings in all, and very few of these fish got to market, owing to a delay in landing and lack of transport facilities. Continuous requests to have a landing slip over the next decade were raised. An editorial in the *Cork Examiner* on 1 July 1926 (p. 14) leads with a request to the Irish Tourism Association to focus their energy on developing tourism in the Barley Cove area:

> Three miles further west from Crookhaven one comes to Barley Cove. To the uninitiated the name probably means nothing, but to anyone who has once been there it conjures up visions of a beach such as all sea lovers dream of and few discover. Unfortunately, as yet Barley Cove does not possess a hotel; there is not even, a village there, but its beach is bounded on the west by the Mizen, on the east by Brow Head, on the north by a charming fresh water lake with Mount Gabriel forming a fitting background for this sea-bather ... There is no

place so eminently suitable for a seaside golf links ... It is greatly to be hoped the Irish Tourist Development Association will soon begin to take an interest in this district ... In the near future we hope to see this district crowded with happy bathers, contented golfers, rapturous artists, tourists of all descriptions awed by its beauty, its inhabitants more prosperous, and the extreme west of our county no longer unknown.

It took several years before the vision of the *Cork Examiner* and others, who articulated one for the area through the work of the Tourism Association, took effect. By 1930 the golf links was in place with further elaboration of it in 1967. On 3 April 1967, the Irish Seascape Hotel and Villas was officially opened by An Taoiseach Jack Lynch and blessed by James Horgan, PP of Goleen.

In July 2000 the chairman of Cork County Council, Mr John Mulvihill, officially launched the council's project for conservation, management and development of the sand dune area in Barleycove. The project began in 1993 when the council initiated the compulsory purchase process to acquire the sand dune area, which measured approximately 100 acres. The dunes themselves, along with the delicate ecosystems that they support, were in danger of being destroyed largely as a result of unrestricted access, especially by its overuse for camping and caravan parking.

The total cost of the project to date, excluding land acquisition, is around £300,000, of which £150,000 was provided from the Tourism Operational Programme with the balance coming from the council's own resources. The development to date consists of the provision of public toilet facilities; a water supply to the beach; and the construction of a boardwalk and pontoon to allow easy access to the beach.

27. A Cul-de-Sac Speaks – Crookhaven and Its Connections

Crookhaven or Cruachan in Irish may mean a little hillock. Through the ages the neighbourhood has always been an important asset to those who controlled it. A Roman Catholic church existed in the area, dedicated to St Molaga, in 1199. The Irish O'Mahony family had a castle there in the fifteenth century. Sir Thomas Crooke was part of an English settlement in Baltimore in the early seventeenth century and might have also influenced the origins of the name Crookhaven. Around 1620 Sir Richard Boyle, the Earl of Cork, and Sir William Hull of Leamcon advanced the development of pilchard fisheries in the sheltered harbour of Crookhaven. In truth, this rural area was of considerable importance as it also had a star-shaped fort to protect it. By the mid-nineteenth century, the adjacent village supported the exportation of wheat, oats, pork and butter, and timber and timber and coal were occasionally imported. Copper mines were worked near the tip of Crookhaven Peninsula.

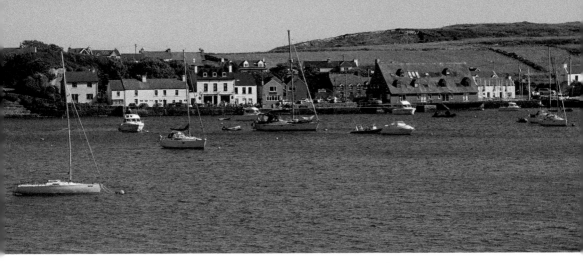

Above and right: Crookhaven.

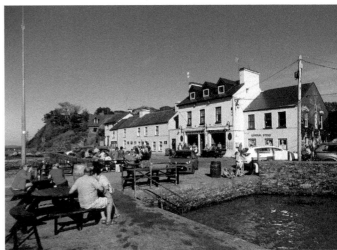

In the mid-nineteenth century, Crookhaven, because of its geographical position, came prominently into the competition between Reuter and the Telegraph companies to speed up the traffic in news across the Atlantic. Both Reuter and *The Times* had by the end of the 1850s special fast steamers to meet the mail boats from America outside Southampton Water. Wooden cylinders containing the American mails were thrown down to them and the two boats then raced for the shore and the London telegraph.

Competition gradually forced the boats further and further out into the Atlantic. Tenders were used to intercept the mail boats at Roche's Point off Cobh; then Reuter laid his own telegraph wire from Cork to Crookhaven and the mails were intercepted off the extreme south-west corner of Ireland. The result of this was that the Reuter messages reached London eight hours ahead of those of the rival firms.

Crookhaven attracted the attention of the famous Italian inventor Guglielmo Marconi (1874–1937) who, in October 1907, successfully conducted field trials in the area at Brow Head, where his wireless station was in operation from June 1901. The West Cork station was one of several he established in other stations around the southern English and Irish coasts. Morse code has been used since 1884 and was initiated by Marconi in 1898 when he transmitted between Ballycastle, County Antrim, and Rathlin Island. That equipment was afterwards moved along the coast to Malin Head and Inishtrahull.

In Crookhaven Marconi arrived himself and he established that morse signals were clearly received from Poldhu in Cornwall, some 225 miles away. This established that the station's range was up to the planned 300 miles using a spark gap transmitter and coherer detectors and now Marconi was confident of 'bridging the Atlantic'.

Apart from Marconi's experimental work as a wireless station the principal activity at Crookhaven was establishing communications with seagoing vessels and most ships coming from the west, bound for European ports, got in contact with Crookhaven so it sprang into prominence. The Crookhaven station started to fade out around 1914 and a station at Valentia Island in County Kerry took over its role.

28. Upon the Ramparts of Ruins – Three Castle Head

Located on a western headland above the Mizen Head is what is known as Three Castle Head. Spectacular in its location, Dun Locha or Dunlough (Fort of the Lake) sits atop the brink of a 100-metre cliff face on the site of an ancient promontory fort. In its day it was an important strategic location with 360-degree views of the landscape. Historical information signs on the approach to the castle point to an annal record that it was constructed by Donagh na Aimrice O'Mahoney, Donagh the Migratory, in 1207. He is reputed be a traveller on pilgrimages to the Holy Land and supposed to be a scholar. Scholars have also noted that the extant ruins are more fifteenth century in date and possibly were added to an earlier structure.

According to the Archaeological Inventory of West Cork, the castle's location is all about creating maximum defence. The three towers of this edifice are connected by a rampart wall of some 20 feet in height, one of the highest medieval walls still

Three Castle Head.

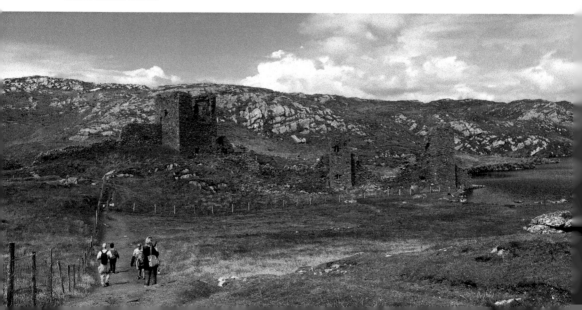

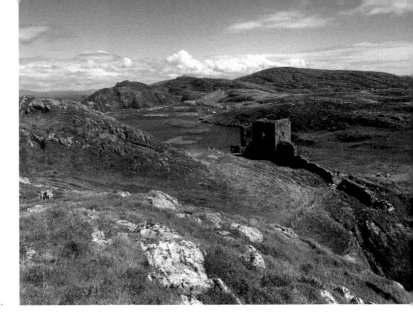

Three Castle Head.

intact in Ireland. Walls extend from the edge of the cliff eastwards to the lake. Dry stone masonry was used in its construction. The geology of the area is metamorphic, which supplied relatively flat and regular stone. Quarried from nearby, the stones were not cut but utilised as they were.

Tower number one by the lake was three storeys high, with a main arched entrance. Tower number two was of a similar height, also with a spiral staircase, and has an interior archway at ground level that led either to a separate room below or was the entrance to a souterrain leading to the sea, utilising the natural crevices in the rock. The third and tallest tower, 10–15 metres in height, also had three storeys. Within its space, the ground floor had several loophole windows. Above the second level are two arches, which support a stone ceiling. It had uppermost ramparts for observation and defence.

There are 40 acres behind the castle known as the Island to explore as well. On foot it is rough terrain but the visitor is met with spectacular views of the Mizen Peninsula and Beara Peninsulas.

29. Ireland's Southern Point – Mizen Head

In 1903, it was decided to build Mizen Head Fog Signal Station on Cloghane Island, and three years later the project was established. In bad visual conditions, the keeper had to manually set off an explosive charge every three minutes to warn shipping. The famous suspension bridge was built between 1908 and 1910 to connect the island with the mainland. In 1931, a wireless beacon was installed at Mizen and in 1959 a light was placed on the rocks at the end of Head at a height of 170 feet, with a range of 13 miles in clear weather. The fog signal was discontinued in the seventies when sonar and satellite navigation took over.

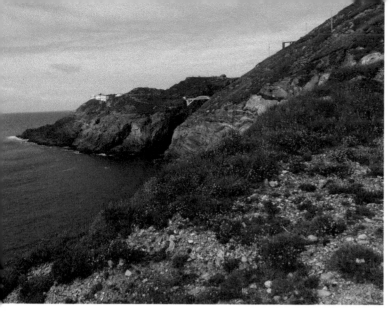

Mizen Head.

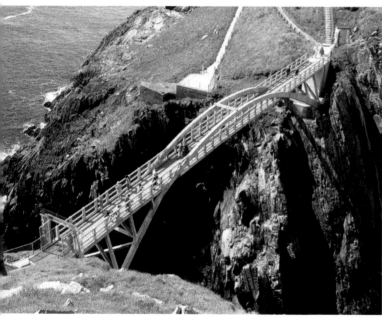

Mizen Head bridge.

In April 1993, the last keepers left Mizen, the station was de-manned and all the equipment was automated. In July that year, the Mizen Tourism Co-Operative Society, a local community group, opened Mizen to the public and created a remarkable visitor centre.

The visitor centre features ninety-nine steps down to the famous suspension bridge, 172 feet across and 150 feet above sea level, from which there are breathtaking views of nearby sheer cliffs and dramatic drops to the ocean. Views of the south and west coasts, not to mention proximity to the majestic Atlantic in its rawest form, combined with the huge cliffs, ravines and crevices against which the sea pounds, make the Mizen experience an unforgettable experience.

A marked and thoroughly safe route leads to the keeper's house and engine room where an official guide awaits to unfold the saga of this fascinating place.

30. A Chequered Past – Bantry House

The elegant Bantry House defines the character of the adjacent local town. The house inspired the town's development and the pier vice-versa. The Archaeological Inventory of West Cork presents research excavations carried out in 2001 in an area directly west of the present house. Here the remains of a site of a deserted Gaelic medieval village and a seventeenth-century English settlement were discovered. Excavations revealed the foundations of the gable end of a mid-seventeenth-century house. This was overlain by a more substantial and better-built rectangular structure, interpreted as a timber-built English administrative building. A palisade trench, dug late in the sixteenth or early in the eighteenth century, immediately predated this building. According to the excavator, this had presumably created a stockade foundation around the early plantation settlement. Sixteenth-century cultivation ridges were also uncovered. These had cut into the foundations of a fifteenth-/sixteenth-century Gaelic domestic structure.

The area seems to have been abandoned in the mid-seventeenth century and all available cartographic and documentary evidence indicated that no further subsequent building or landscaping had taken place. The narrative of the old sites fell out of memory.

The earliest records for the next phase of the site date from around 1690 and describe land deals between Richard White and the Earl of Anglesey, which established the basis of the Bantry House estate. The records, which are in the archives of the library of University College Cork, include information about the ownership of land and property on the family's Bantry, Glengarriff, Castletownbere and Macroom estates. The Whites built a detached five-bay two-storey country house over a basement around 1710.

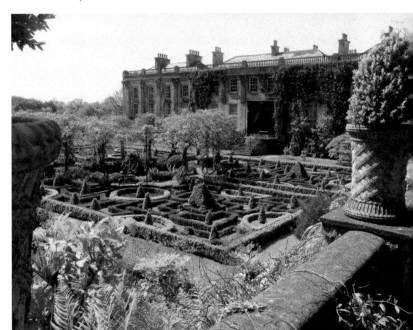

Bantry House.

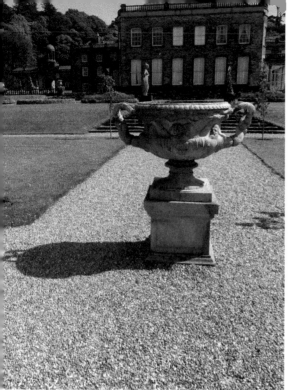

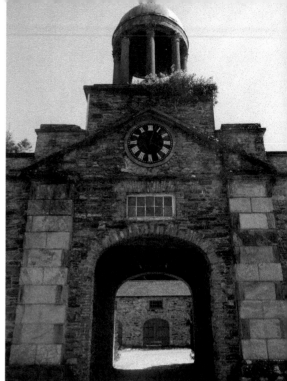

Above left: Bantry House.

Above right: Old stables, Bantry House.

The original structure displays a Queen Anne style, with later Georgian and Victorian elements also present. The architectural designs of the phased construction draw on classical architecture, through ornate porticos, columns and pilasters. The interior fabric is of great significance, including Pompeii tiling, Venetian glass and Italian plasterwork. The building is an outstanding example of the evolution of large country houses through time and it forms part of an interesting complex of demesne related structures with the outbuildings, gate lodges and extensively landscaped gardens.

In 1816, Richard White was created 1st Earl of Bantry. Prior to his marriage, he toured extensively on the European Continent, making sketches of landscapes, vistas, houses and furnishings, which he later used as inspiration in expanding and refurbishing Bantry House. The White family intermarried with other well-known landed families throughout the nineteenth century including the Herberts of Muckross House, Killarney, and the Guinness family of Dublin. Inspired by his travels and contacts, in 1820 Richard invested in the construction of new six-bay two bow-ended additions to the old country house, as well as adding elaborate landscaped gardens complete with outbuildings, stables and gate lodges. In 1845 new bow-ended wings were also added.

William White, the 4th and last Earl of Bantry, died in 1891. Ownership of the estate then passed to his nephew, Edward Leigh, who assumed the additional name of White in 1897. His daughter, Clodagh, inherited Bantry House and estates on the death of her father in 1920, and in 1927, she married Geoffrey Shellswell, who assumed the additional name of White. Clodagh Shellswell-White died in 1978 and the ownership of the house and estate passed on to her son, Egerton Shellswell-White. Today the house and gardens still belong to the White family and are open to the public to explore and engage with.

31. An Expedition into the Past – Stories from Bantry Bay

Bantry Bay sunsets are very beautiful. A gaze around the bay shows inlets and the Caha Mountains looming to the north. The derivation of Bantry is said to have come from Beann, son of Conor Mac Nessa, King of Ulster in the first century. The Vikings first landed in Ireland in AD 836 and shortly afterwards made their first appearance in the Shannon. It is said that they gave the islands Whiddy and Dursey their names, especially the ending in 'ey', which is typical Viking naming.

Fast forward to the sixteenth century and an ancient map of Bantry and Beara shows a small chapel at the north-eastern end of the bay's little Chapel Island. This may be the Church of Iniscuingi that was listed in a decretal letter of 1199, a possession of Gill Abbey in the late medieval period.

A graveyard to the south-west of Bantry nods to the existence of a Franciscan friary, which existed in 1466 and was supressed in 1542. The graveyard has a collection of sixteen late medieval carved fragments, mostly from door and indoor surrounds and parts of cloister arcading. The church was greatly damaged by the English in 1568 and its remains were taken down by Domhnall O'Sullivan Bere in 1602. O'Sullivan Bere family made their presence known by possessing a castle on a rocky outcrop of Whiddy Island. Some walls of this ancient fortification still survive.

Information panels on Bantry's town square champions Ireland's nationalist past and define the layout of the square and which history a visitor engages with first. The panels describe the collective memory of the campaign of Theobald Wolfe Tone in the interests of the United Irishmen and the independence of his country. He journeyed

Bantry Bay.

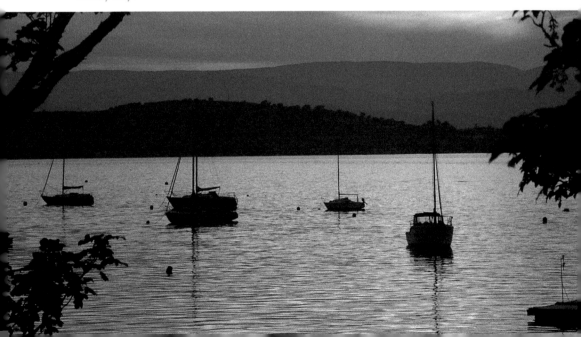

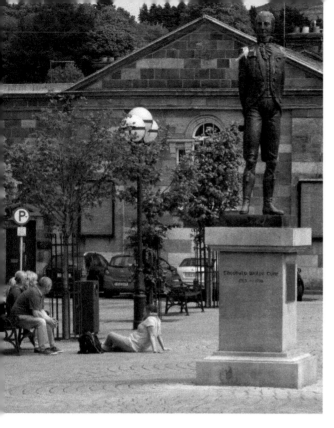

Statue of Theobald Wolfe Tone on Bantry Square.

to Paris at the beginning of 1796 to court the French to help with rebellion against the British in Ireland. There he met General Hoche, the brilliant French commander. On 16 December a fleet of forty-four vessels and 15,000 men under General Hoche and Admiral Morard-de-Galles set sail from Brest.

The expedition was ill-fated from the start, for it was but a day at sea when the frigate *Fraternite* carrying Hoche and Morard-de-Galles got separated from its companions and never reached the Irish shore. A dense fog arose, and Bouvet, the Admiral-in-Command, found he had only eighteen sailing in company. Two days later, however, he had thirty-three, and he steered directly for Cape Clear Island. Land was sighted on the 21st, and though a rough easterly breeze was blowing, sixteen vessels succeeded in gaining Bantry Bay, but twenty remained outside battling hopelessly against the gale and were eventually driven off the coast. A landing was impossible, and Tone, aboard the gunship *Indomitable*, spent his cold Christmas on the bay. On the night of 25 December an order came from Bouvet to cut and put to sea. It was decided to land in the Shannon, but with rough weather increasing, the squadron put to sea and returned to France. It was 27 December and the end of the Bantry Bay expedition. Of the *circa* forty-eight ships that left Brest on 16 December 1796, only thirty-six returned to France. The rest were either captured by the English navy or wrecked.

La Surveillante was considered unseaworthy for the return journey and was scuttled by its crew in Bantry Bay. Its crew and all 600 cavalry and troops on board were transferred safely to other French ships in the fleet. According to the National Wreck Inventory, the three-masted *La Surveillante* was built in Lorient in 1778 and carried thirty-two guns. The vessel had successful naval engagements with British warships during the period of the American War of Independence (1775–82). The wreck of *La Surveillante* was discovered in 1981 during seabed clearance operations following the Betelgeuse oil tanker disaster. One of *La Surveillante*'s anchors had been trawled up by fishermen and put on display in Bantry. In 1987 two 12-pound cannons were raised from the wreck, and in 1997 the ship's bell was lifted, which is now currently on display in Bantry Armada Centre, at Bantry House.

As an additional consequence of the 1796 attempted French invasion, the British government built three batteries on Whiddy Island, which can be explored by taking a ferry to the island. Despite being abandoned in 1807, the middle battery, being the largest and best surviving of the three, is in good condition and showcases a high level of craftsmanship and dominates a vast area of land with commanding views to all sides.

32. A Rugged Walking Trail – The Sheep's Head

Leaving the town, we pass Bantry House, and further on, the Vicarage, where we branch off from the main road and take the thoroughfare skirting the bay nearly the whole distance to Sheep's Head ... the entire extent of Bantry Bay again lies before us in all its varied charms; In some places the altitude is over a thousand feet, and in places it presents the appearance of utter desolation ... by ascending any of these three heights the tourist will be enabled to take in the entire extent of Bantry Bay at a glance. (JP Hayes, Through the Free State, *Southern Star*, 3 August 1929, p. 5)

Mining, begun in Sheep's Head in 1845, opened up access into the heart of the Sheep's Head peninsula. Mines were opened in Gurtavallig, Killeens North, Killeens South, near Bantry and a large mine at Rooska. These mines yielded silver, copper and zinc ore of a very high quality. Roads were required to transport the ore from the northside to Dooneen Pier. It is recorded that a new road, 10 miles long, was

Walking trail at Seefin, Sheep's Head.

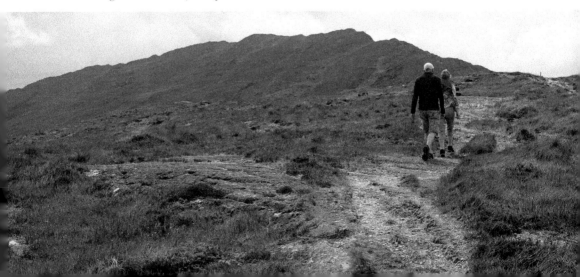

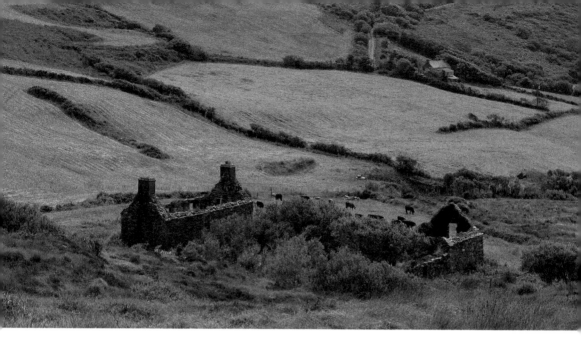

Sheep's Head.

built in ten weeks by hand and was over the Goat's Path track over the mountains. With a lack of venture capital and investment from Westminster, in time the mines eventually closed one by one as the nineteenth century progressed, with the last one closing in 1889.

Fast forward a century and during 1994 preparations began in the Bantry region for the 1996 commemoration of the 1796 Wolfe Tone and French Expedition, a concerted effort was made to develop the potential of the peninsula for business and tourism. The 'blueprint' report, supported by West Cork LEADER and the Armada Centre, contained details of sixteen new events that were likely to significantly extend the tourism season. An advisory committee consisting of representatives from commercial, voluntary and statutory organisations would also be set up. The initiation of a tourist plan aimed to enhance the economic and social well-being of the region. In 1996 President of Ireland Mary Robinson opened up the first of the scenic walking trails. The walk has helped make it one of just four official European Destinations of Excellence in the country.

The Sheep's Head is a mere 25 miles (40 km) long and 2.5 miles (4 km) wide, but the walks and trails, which have been developed by West Cork LEADER, the local community councils, Cork County Council and locals have created one of the best historical trails in the south-west of Ireland. One can crisscross an incredible array of ancient monuments and even modern gems of buildings. Check out the archaeology inventory of West Cork for more and wonder at the array of standing stones and groups, ringforts, promontory forts, an O'Daly and an O'Mahony castle, burial grounds, holy wells, mass rock, old farmsteads, an early nineteenth-century signal tower on Ballyroon Mountain, a miners' settlement and Our Lady Star of the Sea Roman Catholic Church (built in 1897). Don't forget to walk out on the new paths to the tip of the Sheep's Head peninsula, which was constructed as a result of the development of the oil terminal at Whiddy Island. It first exhibited light on 14 October 1968. The lighthouse was monitored by the keepers at Mizen Head Lighthouse until its automation in 1993.

33. The Rugged Glen – Glengarriff and the Caha Pass

Glengarriff, translated from 'An Gleann Garbh' in Irish, means 'The Rugged Glen'. It has been famous as a holiday destination since the 1700s and boomed in the Victorian times as an important stop along the Prince of Wales Grand Tour route. In 1835 Thomas Eccles rented land and buildings, comprising just over 28 acres, from the Earl of Bantry for the sum of £16 12s. As part of this he opened an inn. John Eccles, son of Thomas, carried out a major reconstruction of the inn in 1890 and also changed the name from Glengarriff Inn to the Eccles Hotel. Writer George Bernard Shaw (1856–1950) stayed in the hotel in 1910/1911 and is reputed to have written extensively during his time here. During the 1920s William Butler Yeats (poet and playwright) was a regular visitor to the Eccles Hotel.

Rising from Glengarriff village is the road to the Caha Pass, whose windyness is best captured by this quote in this 1898 guidebook:

> As we proceed the road for some distance is pleasantly diversified, but soon becomes by miniature lakes, streams, barren mountainous districts, and craggy precipices. The grandeur and beauty of this drive will justify the traveller in saying with a celebrated writer, that the attractions of Ireland are kept too silent – in fact, that there is a 'conspiracy of silence' by which the loveliness of the island is kept away from tourists (Glengarriff section, *Guide to the Most Picturesue Tour of Western Europe*, 1898).

At a height of 1,200 feet, the main tunnel is on the Cork–Kerry border and is also known as the Caha Pass. The hand-hewn pass is also located at the scenic border of County Cork and County Kerry. Turner seems to be the local landowner at one time.

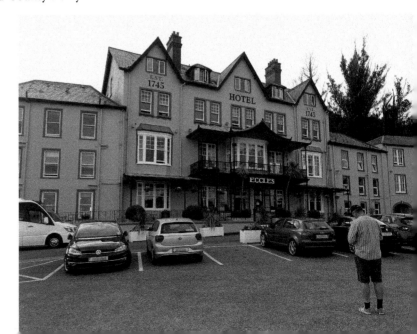

Eccles Hotel, Glengarriff.

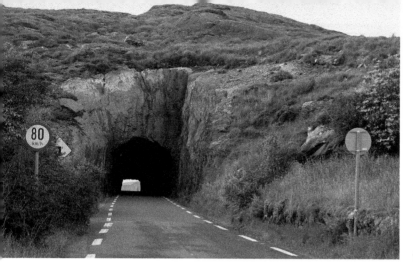

Caha Pass.

On the Kerry side the main tunnel is followed by three more mini-tunnels, a set of twin tunnels and a final short tunnel. These tunnels were constructed as a relief works for local labourers and were meant to open up new tourist routes from the 1830s onwards into south Kerry. One could only imagine the exhilaration of passing through Turner's Tunnel on horse and carriage and later by motor bus.

34. An Island of Curiosities – Garinish Island

Back in Napoleonic days British coastal defences were constructed on the south coast of Ireland to slow down a threatened French invasion. One of the sites of a Martello tower and a fort or barrack building was erected on Garinish Island off Glengarriff. For years after the military had vacated their garrison at Garinish, the island remained unoccupied, but in 1910 it was purchased by a wealthy Belfast man, Annan Bryce. He frequently holidayed in Glengarrife with his wife. Bryce was a Liberal MP for Inverness and his wife – formerly Violet L'Estrange – was a cousin of the Countess Markievicz.

The island was 37 acres in size and consisted of rock gorse and heather, complete with a stretch or two of bog. Mr Bryce decided to plant the island, lay out gardens and build a mansion in keeping with the ornate surroundings. Harold Peto, the noted landscape architect, was engaged on the design. When work commenced around 100 men were engaged in planting shelter belts, digging away bog, blasting rock and building the Italian garden and other ornamental erections.

Pending the building of their mansion the Bryces stayed for long periods in a cottage on the island, watching the development of their plans. Work was halted with the outbreak of the First World War. Annan Bryce's investments suffered severely, expenditure on the island had to be slashed and the idea to build a mansion was abandoned altogether. The plans, however had already been drawn up, and they are preserved in the Office of Public Works. They are the handiwork of a Belfast

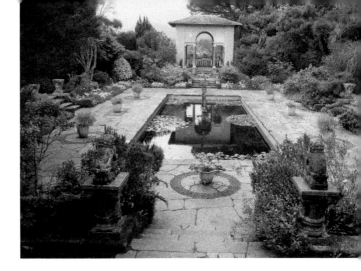

Old Bryce House, Garinish Island.

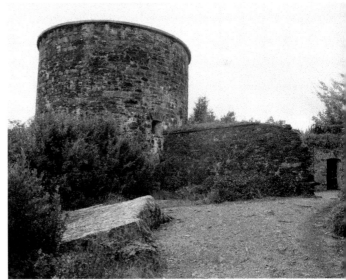

Martello tower, Garinish Island.

architectural firm, McKenzie and Young, and show an elaborate Italianate building in the Baronial style.

The existing Martello tower had been incorporated in the planned building as a circular 'Garden Room', and the old fort was also to have been utilised. The remainder was an ornate structure liberally endowed with balconies, towers, and cloister-like passages. There was a colonnaded terrace leading to the water's edge, and one façade shows a Byzantine tomb in its fabric – one of the many curiosities collected by the owner for the island's embellishment.

Annan Bryce died in 1924, and his widow continued to live in the cottage and develop the gardens to the best of her ability. She survived until 1939, but seven years before her death she handed care of the property over to her son. By then the shelter-belts had reached a stage when it was possible to commence planting the exotic shrubs, which are now a feature of the island. The sheltered situation, the small degree of frost, and the exceptional mildness of the Glengarriff neighbourhood provided an ideal setting for the camellias, the magnolias, and the rhododendrons for which Garnish was to become famous. A few years earlier the Bryces had advertised for a head gardener. The successful applicant was a Scotsman, Murdo McKenzie, who hailed from the Inverness region of Scotland.

Roland Bryce, a brother of Annan Bryce, inherited the island and its curiosities. He was Ambassador to the USA and when he died in 1954, he bequeathed the island to the Irish nation as a botanist's paradise and study hub of sorts. Garinish then became the responsibility of the Office of Public Works, with assistant principal architect Sydney F. Maskell in a supervisory capacity. At this stage the number of visitors stood at approximately 8,000 yearly.

At one time the island was known as Illauncullin, 'The Island of Holly', which was shortened to Ilnacullin. This was the name always used by the Bryces, and that was the name on their notepaper. Through the decades the name has been corrupted to Garnish Island as well.

35. The Border of Counties – The Healy Pass

Almost immediately after crossing the bridge spanning the Adrigole River at Adrigole, the coast road merges with one sweeping down from the north-west, which seems to delve into the very core of the tremendous mountains, whose peaks soar above one another. The road weaves out 'S' hooks, scissors and horseshoe bends as it climbs ever upwards to the Healy Pass, which marks the Cork–Kerry border.

The pass was also the route by which livestock was conveyed, particularly cattle to and from the Kenmare fair. For a long period, it was a mere track beaten out by those following the line of least resistance, and thus, invariably, was identical with the course of mountain torrents, as water always manages to percolate through the easy passages. From time immemorial it was the way used by the local people. Through it the dead were carried on their last journey to the home of their birth. It was the place where the coffins were rested after the arduous climb while those engaged prepared for the even more perilous descent.

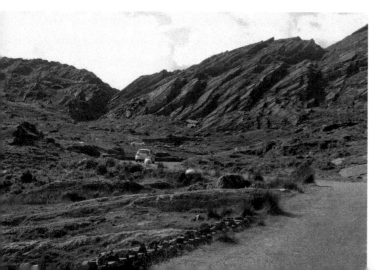

Healy Pass.

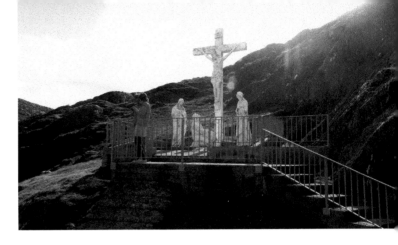

Crucifixion cross,
Healy Pass.

In the closing years of 1890s and the early decade of the twentieth century, Mr Tim Healy, then one of the Irish representatives in the English Parliament at Westminster, fought to have something done to render the pass more passable for the inhabitants on this side of the peninsula. He was, however, thwarted at every turn by powerful vested interests, keen on the preservation of the amenities of certain residential estates on the Cork–Kerry border, which, it was believed, would be impaired if the right of way were put into more frequent use.

Under the Irish Free State Tim Healy did not forget his pet project, and eventually he succeeded in getting the then Minister for Local Government and Public Health, General Richard Mulcahy, to put the long-deferred project into motion. A sum of £7,000 was advanced for the purpose and work began in 1931. Making every allowance for the advance in engineering knowledge and skill and the up-to-date equipment, it was nevertheless a herculean task. A makeshift roadway existed as far as the point where the rise began, but from that onwards it was practically virgin country. In 1932 the feat was accomplished. Operations were continued down the other side for a distance of a mile and a half into County Kerry until contact was established with an existing road there.

Before leaving Healy's Pass mention must be made of the magnificent wayside calvary, which was unveiled in early June 1935. Made of marble, it is sheltered in a niche within a few yards of the highest point of the roadway. It was the gift of a Cork City donor who wished to remain anonymous.

36. The Manouevres of Time – Castletownbere and Berehaven

During his travels in County Cork's most westerly peninsula, Beara, in 1750, Charles Smith wrote 'Castletown, alias Castledermot, is a small village of little note, opposite to the island of Berehaven'. In 1758, Pococke, who travelled by sea from Bantry to Berehaven Harbour, wrote: 'There is no village at this harbour, only small houses'.

Not far from the eastern entrance of Berehaven a portion of the French fleet anchored in 1796, with the object of landing an invading force, but like the Spanish Armada, the elements defeated them. The French ships had to cut their cables,

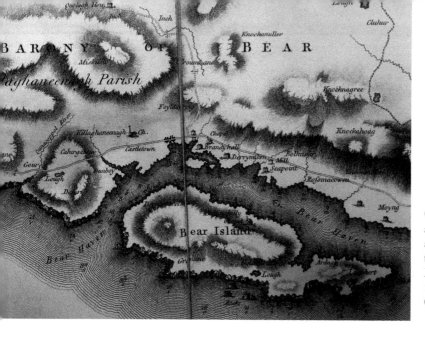

Castletownbere and Bere Island, as depicted on the Grand Jury Map of Cork, 1811. (Cork City Library)

leaving their anchors in the bottom, where they were a source of trouble to the fishermen, whose nets are sometimes damaged by them. After the attempted French invasion seven forts or redoubts were erected on Bere Island.

The strategical importance of Berehaven Harbour, with its 7-mile-long and 1.5-mile-wide anchorage, was acknowledged by the naval and military authorities of Great Britain in the nineteenth century. In the despatches of the Duke of Wellington, published after his death, he made strong recommendations in favour of making Berehaven a naval station in the Atlantic, and connecting it with Dublin by railway. This was in the days when railway construction was only commencing, and after sixty years the railway was still 30 miles short of the goal recommended by the Iron Duke.

The large British military and naval base on Bere Island during the nineteenth century and through the period of the First World War provided a period of economic prosperity in Castletownbere. Through exploring the architecture of the shopfronts of the main streets and laneways of Castletownbere investment in the physical fabric of the streetscape can be seen clearly from the mid nineteenth century. An old convent dates to around 1880 while the Gothic Revival-style Church of Ireland was built around 1860, with the Gothic Revival Roman Catholic Sacred Heart Church built in 1907.

An account in the *Skibbereen Eagle* newspaper on 4 May 1907 (p. 11) recorded of Castletownbere:

At the entrance of Bantry Bay, with its sixteen hundred inhabitants is in many respects one of the most interesting towns in Cork County, as it is one of the most thriving and progressive. No doubt its prosperity is chiefly due to the fact that during the naval manoeuvres every year it is one of the bases, and the numerous battleships and cruisers that visit the bay bring thousands of pounds sterling into the pockets of the townspeople. And year after year it is becoming more important as a naval station. This year it is to be visited by four fleets, and during the winter and spring months the Admiralty have spent much money in erecting stores, drill sheds, etc.

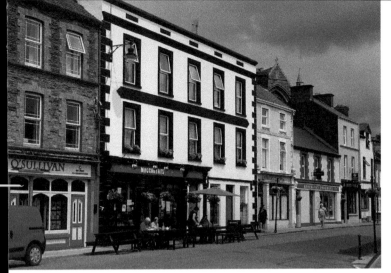

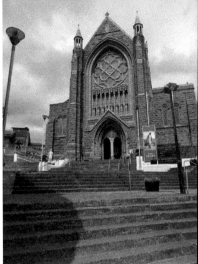

Above left: MacCarthy's in Castletownbere.

Above right: Sacred Heart Church, Castletownbere.

In the 1960s Castletownbere Harbour was developed as the major fishing port for the south-west Ireland. Several fish-processing plants can still be seen in its pier area.

Also check out MacCarthy's bar where one can find out about the life and times of Aidan McCarthy and his Japanese sword. Training as a doctor at University College Cork (UCC), he survived some of the most harrowing events of the Second World War. Aidan received the sword as a gift from the commandant of a Nagasaki prison camp, Second Lieutenant Isao Kusuno, whom Aidan saved from a lynching by prisoners after the A-bomb was dropped in August 1945. The sword is on display in MacCarthy's.

37. A Monument of Initiative – Bere Island Heritage Centre

Opened in October 2010, President McAleese congratulated the 200-strong community at Bere Island for its determination in obtaining funding for the project, saying the building was a monument to their initiative. Funding for the centre was acquired from the Department of the Islands, Cork County Council and an EU Island Community fund. Bere Island Heritage Centre is a centrepiece and is housed in the Ballinakilla Old School building (built in 1857) on Bere Island in West Cork. This gem of a heritage centre champions information on genealogy, hosts the St Michael's graveyard database and information on the island's heritage sites and walks. Traditional skills workshops, meditation retreats, school tours and craft fairs are regularly arranged in the meeting rooms.

On the panels within the centre and on historical information panels across the island, the island's story is told. Fortification and defence define the history and community of the island especially in the nineteenth century.

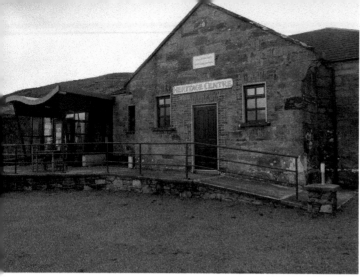

Bere Island Heritage Centre.

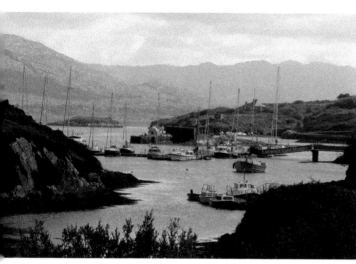

Lawrence Cove, Bere Island.

It was on 1 January 1810 that Robert Hedges Eyre and Thomas Leahy leased to Brigadier General Benjamin Fisher, representing the Board of Ordnance, around 47 acres for the building of a barracks for 900 years at a rent of £3 8s 3d at the East End of Bere Island. In addition on 1 January 1810 Daniel O'Sullivan, Murtagh O'Sullivan, John Lavallin Puxley and Robert Hedges Eyre leased to Brigadier General Fisher a plot of ground for the building of a redoubt at the western end of the Island for 900 years at a rent of £8 8s 3d. Two impregnable modern fortifications with guns now commanded the western and eastern entrances to the harbour. Five Martello towers were also built across the Island on the western and eastern points.

Bere Island formed a part of the White estate until 1853 when it was purchased by the Englishman Lord Charles Pelham Clinton from Richard White, Earl of Bantry.

The government steamer *General McHardy* was launched with another called the *Jackdaw*, which had a crew of three Bere Island men, Dan O'Leary, Jim 'Shonish' O'Sullivan, and Mike Óg O'Sullivan, and plied between Castletownbere and Bere Island, making two trips a day. Their mission was to maintain uninterrupted communication with the mainland, to carry mail and supplies, and to attend to the commands of the army officer in charge.

By the early twentieth century islanders numbered over a thousand, plus the several thousands of British soldiers who were stationed there. The British pulled out in 1938 and handed the camp over to the Irish army, but the Irish pulled out in 1948, closed the camp and buildings and left the islanders stranded and their means of employment gone after more than a century. In recent years, the population has remained steady at around 200. It has two small ferry companies and the community has created an interest in tourism development through sites such as the heritage centre and the impressive Lawrence Cove Marina for boats and yachts, as well as a myriad of walking trails, which peel back the more ancient layers of the island.

38. A Memory of Irish History – Dunboy Castle

The impact of the president of the Munster Plantation, George Carew, in the late sixteenth century, was vast. By the spring of 1586 Carew had been knighted and was sent on a private mission by Elizabeth I to Ireland. Carew arrived into a country where huge tracts of the Earl of Desmond's lands in Munster had been taken over by the English crown. Around 300,000 acres of land were confiscated in total. From 1585, the plantation of Munster had begun and new English settlers were given land. As a reward for Carew's loyalty, he acquired large estates.

George Carew's rise in political circles and in English power structures in Ireland was quick. In February 1588 Carew was appointed Master of the Ordnance and returned to Ireland. In 1590 he was admitted to the Privy Council. Two years later, in 1592, he was made Lieutenant-General of the English Ordnance, and in 1596 and 1597 he was engaged with Essex and Raleigh in expeditions against Spain. In March 1599 he was appointed to attend the Earl of Essex's visit to Ireland and on 27 January 1600 he was made President of Munster. Carew's proceedings for the next three years during his term as president are carefully detailed in *Pacata Hibernia* (1633), nominally

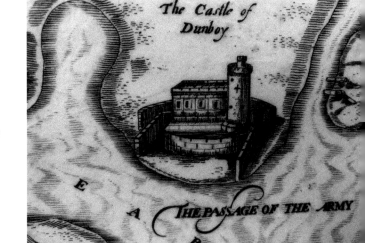

Dunboy Castle, *c.* 1600, by George Carew, president of the English Munster Plantation.

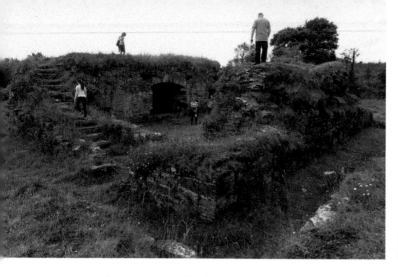

Ruins of Dunboy Castle.

written by Thomas Stafford, but inspired by himself. His win at the Battle of Kinsale in 1601 features prominently in his pages on campaigns in Cork.

Dunboy Castle in Castletownbere was not given up without a fight. In April 1602 Carew took Dunboy Castle and estate, which was the stronghold of the O'Sullivan Bere clan and built to guard the harbour of Berehaven. The O'Sullivan Beres controlled the fishing fleets off the Irish coast and became rich through the collection of taxes on the rights of passage. Dunboy was surrendered to the Spaniards during their invasion of Ireland in 1601 by its owner, Daniel O'Sullivan. Early the next year following the treaty at Kinsale the Irish clan retook the castle by surprise and seized the arms and ammunition the Spaniards had deposited there. Sir George Carew, as well as 5,000 soldiers, were sent to suppress the O'Sullivan Bere. In April, the English army marched against the O'Sullivans to Bantry, and on 6 June set up camp on the opposite side of the castle's bay.

Dunboy Castle was considered impregnable and was only defended by 143 men under the command of Richard McGeoghegan. It took two weeks to take it during which it was almost destroyed by artillery fire. After hand-to-hand fighting the remaining fifty-eight survivors were executed in the town square. The entire castle site lay in ruins until 1730 when the Puxley family was granted the Dunboy estate along with land belonging to the O'Sullivans. They then set about building a mansion close to the Puxley Castle keep and Dunboy Castle was left in ruins. Very little now remains of the old castle. It now comprises of just a few collections of stones, which in parts are almost completely covered with overgrowth.

39. A Ruin of a Ruin – Puxley's Mansion

The ruins of Puxley's Mansion now stand adjacent to Dunboy Castle – a ruin of a ruin in a sense because of unfinished renovations in modern times. The Puxleys probably came from England with Cromwell and settled in County Galway in the seventeenth century. Henry Puxley lived in Ahascragh, County Galway, and his two sons, Henry and John, moved to Castletownbere and built the first section (the western third) of the eventual building. The younger Henry left Dunboy and returned to Galway. John remained on and went into a profitable partnership with the local O'Sullivans in smuggling, exporting wool and importing brandy, tobacco and wine.

John died of a fall from a horse, and his successor was his son, John Lavallin (1772–1856). John Lavallin was to form the company that opened the Castletownbere mines in 1812. Around 1821, he extended the mansion, adding the central part of the present building to accommodate his growing family (his wife Sarah, née Hobbs, of Bantry was to give birth to two sons and six daughters soon after their marriage in 1796).

John Lavallin spent forty-four years working the Berehaven mines. On John Lavallin's death in 1856, the mansion passed to his grandson, John Simon Lavallin Puxley (1831–60), but the grandson was to survive his grandfather for only four years. His brother, Henry Lavallin Puxley (1834–1909), succeeded him. He started building the last section (eastern) of the mansion around 1867. He sold the family shares in the Berehaven mining company in 1869. Henry Lavillin had eight children,

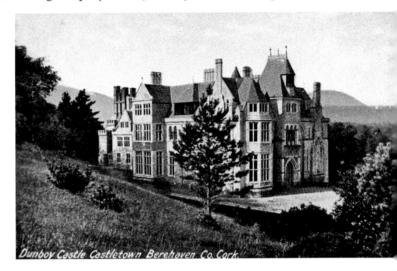

Puxley's Mansion, c. 1900.

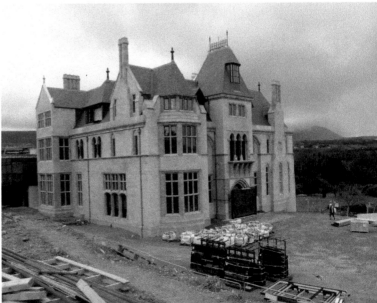

Puxley's Mansion during renovation, February 2008.

but at this stage he had little or no business interests in the Castletownbere area and they lived mainly in Cornwall, the family commuting to West Cork mostly for holidays only. They lived in the western section on their visits. The last section of the mansion took about thirty years to construct.

Henry Lavallin was deeply traumatised by the death of his wife. After her passing work on the mansion ceased. The main hall lacked a staircase, and statues and ornaments imported from Italy were never unpacked.

The castle passed into the possession of the grandson of the original owner, also named Mr Henry Lavallin Puxley. Destruction started by fire took place on Wednesday 8 June 1921 from the Irish Republican Army. In 1926 Henry gave instructions to William G. Wood & Sons, auctioneers in Cork, to sell the estate of the famous Dunboy Castle and around 215 acres of demesne lands. However, the mansion was not redeveloped.

Purchased by four local businessmen in 1999, the mansion was to be redeveloped, in partnership with a large professional hotel group, into an exquisite hotel. Renovation work on the mansion, due to open in 2009, was almost completed but work was suspended in early 2010 following Ireland's economic crash. Today the house remains a ruin of the modern Irish economic history, awaiting redevelopment once again.

40. The Shaper of the Land – The Hag of Beara

Indented by an exposed coastline and defined by the Slieve Mikish and Caha Mountains, the Beara Peninsula is some 45 kilometres long and 15 kilometres wide at its widest point. The principal point in the Caha Range, Hungry Hill stands 2,251 feet and is well known to tourists not only for its mountain lakes and lofty waterfall, but also for the superb view that it affords.

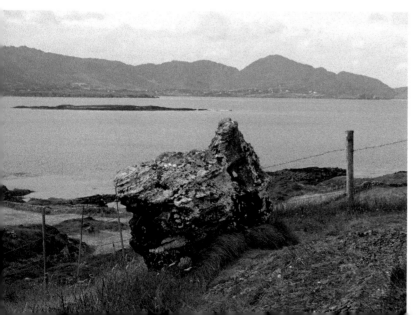

The Hag of Beara.

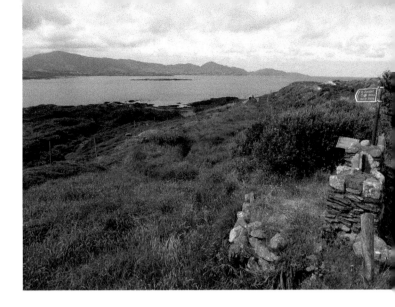

The Hag of Beara.

Prehistoric settlers were attracted to the area as evidenced by standing stones, stone circles and wedge tombs. Rich folklore embedded into the local landscape survives of giants, Spanish princesses and witch-like creatures. The geomorphology of Coulagh Bay is attributed to a pair of fighting giants called the formorians. According to folklore the name Beara is that of a Spanish princess, the wife of Eoghan Mór, mythical second-century King of Munster. Christian tradition pitches the presence of a Celtic Goddess of Harvest, Shaper and Protectoress of the Land – An Chaileach Bhearra, 'the Hag of Beara'. In truth, she represents many cultural meanings such as mother and fertility goddess and divine hag. She was deemed a goddess of sovereignty, who gave the kings the right to rule their lands.

According to the local information sign, the Hag of Beara is associated with the Kilcatherine in the northern part of the peninsula, north of Eyeries, overlooking Coulagh Bay. According to myth, she lived for seven periods of youth one after another – so that every man who co-habited with her came to die of old age. She had so many grandsons and great-grandsons that they made up entire tribes and races – hence her legend is woven into folklore across parts of Ireland and across the west coast of Scotland.

The advent of the arrival of St Caitiarin and Christianity was deemed a threat to her powers. Local folklore has it that one day after collecting seawood along the shore of Whiddy Island, the hag, on her return, encountered the priest asleep on a local hillock. She drew near to him and quietly took his prayer book and ran off. A cripple who lived nearby, on seeing what happened, shouted at the saint, who awoke startled and saw the hag running off. The saint caught up with her, reacquired the prayer book and turned her into a grey pillar stone with her back to the hill and her face to the sea.

Visiting the pillar stone today, the visitor can see offerings of coins and pebbles. The first extant written mention of the hag is in the twelfth-century *Vision of Mac Conglinne*, in which she is named as the 'White Nun of Beare'.

The myth of the hag is harnessed as a construct in forging a national and cultural identity in the early twentieth century. She is mentioned in work by Irish academic, scholar of the Irish language, and politician Douglas Hyde in 1901 and in verse by writer, republican political activist and revolutionary Pádraig Pearse: 'Mise Éire Siné mé ná an Cailleach Béara'. In most recent years, the myth of the hag has been spotlighted again by well-known Irish poet Leanne O'Sullivan.

41. Beneath the Landscape – Allihies Copper Mine Museum

In September 2007 President Mary McAleese opened a Copper Mine Museum in the Old Methodist Church in Allihies. The story boards in the museum come under the general headings of prehistoric mining, nineteenth century mining techniques, geology and various aspects of social history, all of which are explored in an engaging and interconnecting way. The display has a strong visual emphasis and uses good photographs, illustrations, original drawings, diagrams and maps, as well as a number of surviving artefacts.

The copper mines at Allihies ranked among the most important resources of the Beara Peninsula. They are part of the traditions and history of Berehaven. In 1970 the Office of Public Works issued a Preservation Order, under the National Monuments Act, giving full legal protection to a group of Bronze Age copper mines located along the eastern slopes of Mount Gabriel, Schull, County Cork. Researchers have shown that these sites are among the oldest and best surviving prehistoric copper mines in north-west Europe.

It was not until the eighteenth and nineteenth centuries that minerals, chiefly copper, received serious attention. The Allihies Copper Mines at Dooneen were discovered by a Colonel Hall in 1810 and were opened in 1812. The money for the opening of the mines was raised by John Puxley. Dooneen mine, which was abandoned in 1863 probably because of flooding as the shafts were under the sea. Puxley sold the mines between 1863 and 1867 for £100,000 and a royalty of five per cent of output. They were bought by a Dublin company.

Allihies Mines employed a great many people, at the peak of their prosperity, which varied in date from mine to mine. Dooneen, Coom, Old Kealogue, New Kealogue, and others employed around 2,000 men, women and children. Women and girls helped with the washing of the ore and got 3*d* or 4*d* a day, boys got 6*d*, and men 1*s* to 1*s* 4*d*. Even skilled men and miners were rarely paid more than this,

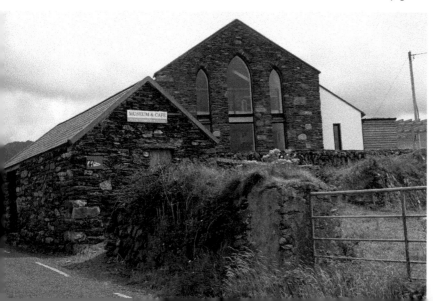

Copper Mine Museum Allihies.

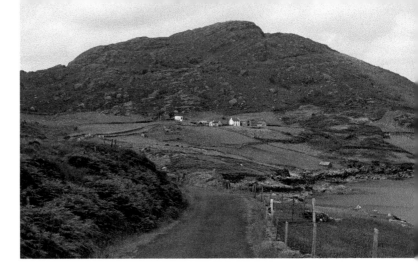

North of Allihies,
Beara Peninsula.

but a heavy price was paid for the prosperity of the district in terms of human lives lost in such a dangerous underground occupation.

In 1869 Puxley sold his mine to the Berehaven Mining Company Ltd. It was later incorporated with the Mining Company of Ireland. This company went into voluntary liquidation in 1885 and there was no activity at the mines during most of the 1890s. In the meantime, many of the unemployed workers went to mines in Calument, Michigan, and many later moved to Butte, Montana.

In 1928 the mines were purchased by a company known as the Allihies Copper Mines Ltd, which was set up in October 1919 by the Kelly brothers of Dublin and Fredrick Rycroft of London. Later, the Kelly Brothers sold their interest in the company to the British Non-ferrous Metal Corporation, which was described as one of the largest mining combines in the world. In 1930 it was reported that the mines were working at a great loss and in June that year they were closed. The closure put over 200 men out of work.

Between 1956 and 1962, exploration work was again carried out at the mines, this time by a largely Canadian-owned company called the Emerald Isle Mining Company. Although the mines were soon deemed to be economically unviable, they provided employment for a number of locals for a time. The mines closed for the last time in 1962 when it was concluded that there was too little copper left for its retrieval to be viable.

Fast forward to November 2002 and conservation work began on part of the old copper mine. Described as an 'internationally unique building', the cost of conserving was estimated at between €300,000 and €400,000. The work was undertaken in a series of phases, the pace of which was determined by availability of funds. The first phase of the conservation work led by a team of specialist builders and stonemasons from Darrock and Brown Ltd of Cornwall.

The conservation work was carried out on the building containing the mine's 'man engine' – an unusual piece of machinery designed to allow miners descend rapidly into the mine. Constructed in Cornwall, England, the machinery consisted of a long wooden rod extended down the length of the shaft, which measured over 1,000 feet. The rod was powered by a steam engine on the surface and moved up and down with each stroke of the engine. Timber steps were attached to the rod, allowing miners to step on and be lifted the distance of the stroke.

Fewer than twenty Cornish Man Engines were ever constructed in the world. The vast majority of them stayed in Cornwall, while the remainder were sold to mines in South Australia, the Isle of Man and Ireland.

42. Crossing a Sound – Dursey Island and Its Cable Car

Though hardly 300 yards wide, the Dursey Sound regularly defied the hardiest boatmen as bad weather swept in and the island was completely cut off. In winter months the islanders could be cut off from supplies and mails, or contact with a priest or doctor, for a week or two as the crossing of Dursey Sound was very dangerous in bad weather. The island experienced a high rate of emigration. Mail was irregular, and horses and cattle had to swim out for the fairs, many drowning while going across the whirlpools. Another story is told of a funeral and that an empty coffin coming from the mainland to the island had to be thrown into the water and the boat towing it across had to he rowed around for half the day as the boatman could not land. Late in the evening the coffin and the boat had to be hauled up the side of a cliff on to the island.

In February 1940, the completion of telephonic communication between Garnish Post Office and Dursey Post Office removed a heavy handicap from the inhabitants of the island and afforded them the means of saving hours in case of urgent need for the services of a doctor or priest, etc. The overhead wire led from a 40-foot pine mast on the mainland to a similar one on the island, the wire being around 60 feet high above the intervening span of 170 yards of water. The work, which was of a very technical and intricate nature, was carried out under the supervision of Mr J. J. Hartnett of the Engineering Department of Cork Post Office. Other plans at the time included consideration for a sheltered landing on the Dursey side with vertical iron stanchions inserted on the mainland landings so that ropes could be used as checkers on boats landing in disturbed seas.

For some time, it was thought that it could be possible to build a bridge across the Sound, but the general consensus thought it would cost too much. In the mid to late 1960s pressure from the local community and the local parish priest, Fr M. Keane, led to a creative engineering solution – that of a cable car project.

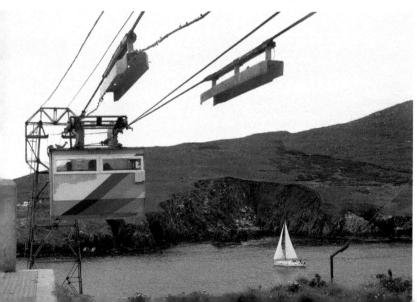

Dursey Island cable car.

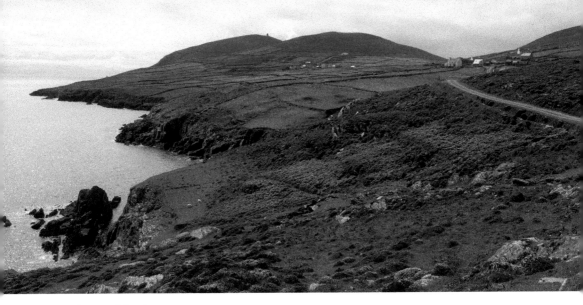

Dursey Island.

The civil engineering side of the work was carried out by the Cork County Council staff, employing local labour. County Council Manager Michael Conlon and West Cork Development team drove the project. The erection of the mechanical plant was executed by four members of the staff of British Chairlifts Ltd, a subsidiary of British Ropeway Engineering.

On 12 December 1969 the official opening by An Taoiseach Jack Lynch took place. The cable-car facility stretchied into Dursey Island high over the ill-famed turbulent sound. The cabin took approximately five to ten minutes to cross the channel and aimed to carry six persons or one cow, and no more than 1,200 lbs on each trip. Over the years, the cable-car facility has been revamped as well as the cabin, with a new car installed in 2019.

43. A Crossroads in the Landscape – Tales from Drimoleague

Drimoleague forms an important access point to the region of West Cork, a junction for the roads extending from Cork to Bantry and Skibbereen. One of the oldest sites associated with Drimoleague is Castledonovan, a tower house that forms a landmark north of the town. It was built by Domhnaill na Croiceann (of the hides) O'Donovan sometime between 1560 and 1584, and possibly on the site of an earlier structure. It was surrendered to the English government in 1592 by his son Donal II. It was regranted to him in 1616, as well as other property and additional legal rights. The building was renovated in the 1620s, and stone dated 1626 in a window

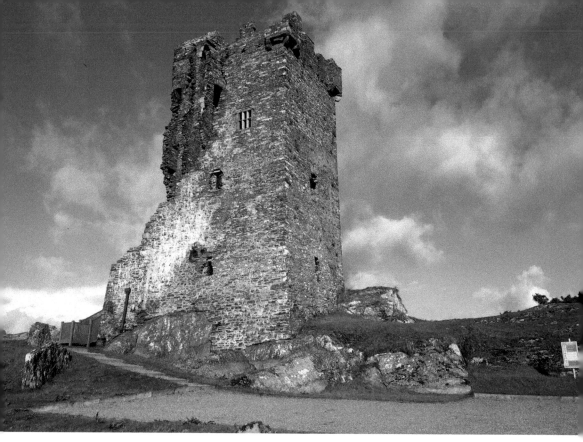

Above: Castle Donovan.

Below: Postcard of Drimoleague Railway terminus. (Cork City Museum)

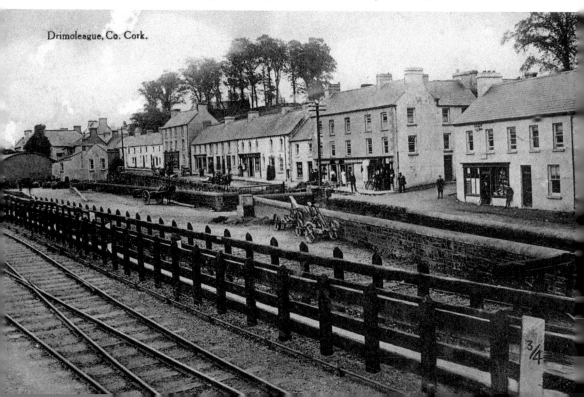

Drimoleague, Co. Cork.

embrasure within the castle. In 1650 the castle was attacked by Cromwellian forces. It was confiscated again in 1654 and granted to Lieutenant Nathaniel Evanson of the Cromwellian army. Local information recalls that the south-west portion of the tower house collapsed in December 1936. In 2000, the tower house was taken into state care.

The O'Donovans attained the first patent for Drimoleague's Fair. The fair in the nineteenth century was remembered as the site of faction fights that took the place of organised sport in West Cork long ago. The fights were finally finished in 1864 when appeals were made to the general public to pool their energies for the good of their country rather than fighting with each other.

In truth Drimoleague village was originally situated around the rock of the castle. On 21 July 1877 the first train arrived in a small hamlet south of the castle and it was this small settlement that became the focus of larger settlement. The Ilen Valley Railway Company influenced the extension from Dunmanway through Drimoleague to Skibbereen. Later in 1881 another branch line was added from Drimoleague to Bantry. With three platforms, it also had a goods platform and cattle pens. Much of the economic life of the rail line was based on milk, butter, flax and grain. The railway encouraged better production and speedier access to wider markets. For eighty years the railway line flourished. However, an economic viability investigation by the government of the day led to the closure of the entire West Cork Railway line on 31 March 1961.

44. A Silver Cup of Gratitude – Dunmanway and Sam Maguire

In the beautiful town of Dunmanway a statue in the town square commemorates the life and times of Sam Maguire, a West Cork man and a patriot from the same county as Jeremiah O'Donovan Rossa, who was an active worker in the National Cause from 1916 to 1921. He did great organisation work in England, was connected with the Irish Republican Brotherhood, was chairman of the London County Board GAA and captain of the London Irish football team and the All-Ireland Gaelic Football Cup is named after him.

Sam was born in Mallabraca, in a beautiful rugged valley 2 miles outside Dunmanway, in 1878. Nothing exists of his birthplace today except an old shell of a cottage with crumbling walls. It is signposted on the main Macroom-Dunmanway road. A memorial sits on the site declaring bluntly: 'Erected to the memory of Sam Maguire. Native of this Place. The All-Ireland Senior Football Cup perpetuates his name'.

Sam Maguire went to the Model School in Dunmanway and later got a job in the post office in London, where his workmates included Michael Collins, Peadar Kearney and Liam McCarthy (of the All-Ireland hurling cup).

Sam Maguire quickly founded the Hibernians senior football club, which represented London in the All-Ireland final in 1900, 1902 and 1903. As his playing days came to an end, Sam got involved in the official side of the GAA and rose to become chairman of the London County Board.

At the same time, under the influence of Michael Collins, Sam got wrapped up in the activities of the Irish Republican Army. As Chief Intelligence Officer, he was a trusted and loyal friend of Collins. Sam died on 6 February 1927, and is buried in St Mary's Churchyard in Dunmanway.

After his death, compatriots of Sam established an appeal for funds for a memorial to his memory. Over a year later a magnificent trophy was commissioned and this was to become a perpetual trophy for the All-Ireland Football final. The trophy was an enlarged replica of the Ardagh Chalice and was elaborately decorated with Celtic ornamentation, the gold centrepiece of which bears a bust of Sam Maguire. In August and early September 1928, the cup, which was made at Messrs Hopkins and Hopkins, O'Connell Street, Dublin, was exhibited to the general public. It was made of approximately 200 ounces of solid silver and was one of the finest specimens of silversmiths' art produced in Ireland. On 17 September 1928 the trophy was

Statue of Sam Maguire, Dunmanway Square.

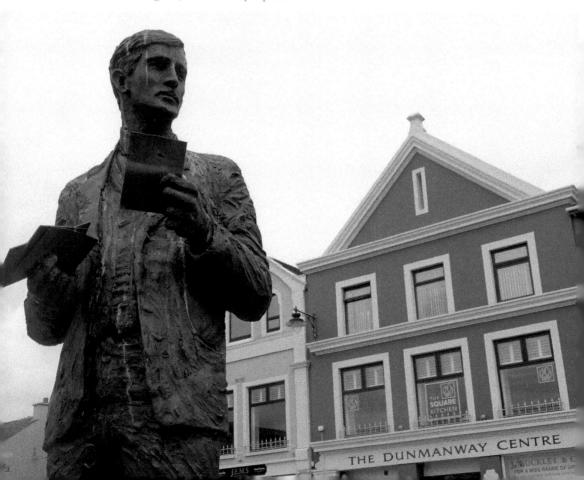

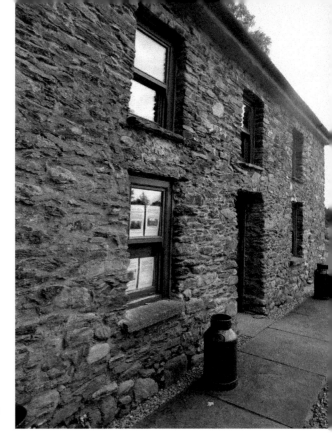

Renovated farmstead marking the birthplace of Sam Maguire.

presented to the GAA for competition by Dr Mark Ryan, president of Sam Magure Memorial Committee. Ten years later the committee was fundraising again – this time for a Sam Maguire playing pitch in Dunmanway.

The first team to win the cup was Kildare when they beat Cavan by a point in the final in 1928. In 1960, Down footballers were the first northerners to win the All-Ireland and take Sam across the border. Later that year, in a kind gesture, the team visited Dunmanway to visit Maguire's birthplace and meet with his elderly sister, Mary.

The trophy was replaced in 1987 after nearly sixty years of wear and tear from jubilant players and supporters had finally taken its toll. Meath captain Mick Lyons hoisted the old Sam Maguire Cup for the last time in 1987 and, twelve months later, was back again to win the new cup.

On 15 September 2002, a statue of Sam Maguire was unveiled as the centrepiece of a new €500,000 plaza in Dunmanway's town centre called Sam Maguire Square. The commission to create a lifesize sculpture commemorating Sam Maguire had been initiated by Cork County Council in response to local requests to create a memorial to this important figure in Irish cultural history. The commissioned artist was Maurice Harron. At that time he divided his time between Derry and Letterkenny, where he had established a bronze foundry. He had many public commissions in Ireland, the UK and North America. Among his best-known works is the sculpture *Hands of Friendship* in Carlisle Square, Derry, the five-figure group entitled *The Hiring Fair* in Letterkenny and *The Irish Famine and Emigration* sculpture in Cambridge, Massachusetts, USA. Also check out the newly launched Sam Maguire heritage trail and around the town and surrounding areas.

45. A Personalised Past – Ballinacarriga Castle

The four-storey Ballinacarriga Castle, adjacent to Ballinacarriga village, is very accessible. Built on a rocky outcrop sometime in the sixteenth century, the castle is associated with the Hurley family. In 1585 Randal Hurley married Catherine Cullinane and their marriage is commemorated on the inside of one of the fourth-storey windows. The arched door and the cut cornerstones have long since disappeared, being appropriated for the construction of a mill that has since been demolished. The castle contained a great hall resting on an arched floor, which was lit by two ornamental windows, the casing of which still exists. The south window has carved figures that seem to represent figures at Crucifixion. One is clad in ecclesiastical garb, the palms of the hands extended, and one supports the shaft of a cross.

There are also Instruments of the Passion, and figures which may represent St John, the Blessed Virgin and St Paul, as well as decorative panels. On the first floor, there are carvings of a figure and five rosettes said to represent Catherine O'Cullane and her children. On the third floor are carvings, which include the inscription '1585 R.M.C.C.' (Randal Muirhily (Hurley) and his wife Catherine O'Cullane).

Below left: Ballinacarriga Castle.

Below right: Sheela-Na-Gig Ballinacarriga Castle.

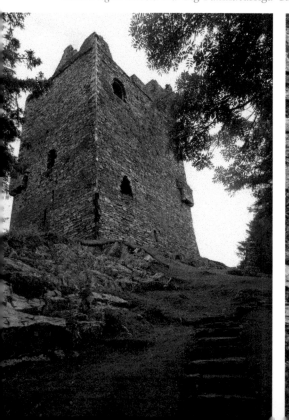
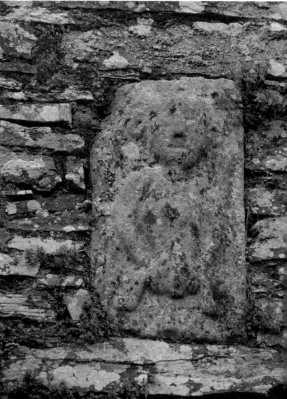

On the external face of the eastern wall of the castle is inserted a carved stone, bearing a representation of one of those grotesque figures known as Sheela-na-gig. Sheela-na-gigs are figurative carvings of naked women exhibiting an embellished vulva. They are architectural grotesques found all over Europe on castles, cathedrals and other buildings. The highest concentrations can be found in Ireland, Great Britain, France and Spain, sometimes together with male figures. Ireland has the greatest number of surviving Sheela-na-gig carvings. There are around ten examples in Ireland. The carvings could have been utilised to protect against demons, death and evil. They are often positioned over doors or windows, presumably to protect these openings.

The Ballabuidhe Horse Fair dates back to 1615, when a charter for it was granted by James I to Randal Óg Hurley of the castle. The fair is steeped in history, tradition and antiquity. It is still one of Ireland's greatest annual horse fairs, to be held on the streets, and where buyers come from all over Ireland and cross-Channel too. Every year horse racing is also held just before the event.

46. Of Saints and Scholars – Kinneigh Round Tower

The town land of Kinneigh is situated 3 miles north-west of Enniskeane and just south of Coppeen. The area is blessed with strong historical societies and local historians, whose writings have survived for over 100 years and have covered many historical gems. One such ancient site, which as a topic has been pursued at length, is the local ancient monastery of Kinneigh. According to the Annals of Cork a see was founded here in AD 611 by St Colman, and the Four Masters record the death of Abbot Forbasach in AD 850. The monastery was beautifully situated on the gentle slope of a hill, being sheltered from the north and east winds. The meaning of the word Kinneigh is uncertain. Some writers in the past record 'Ceann Eich' as meaning 'horse's head' and may connect to the resemblance of the hill to the head of that animal. There is now no hill or rock in the district to support this derivation.

In the tenth century, the old monastery at Kinneigh was abandoned and it appears that the monks, for strategic reasons, selected Sleenoge, half a mile to the east, as the place for their new home. There is no reference to buildings that they erected here except for the round tower, which was constructed in 1014.

There is a remarkable similarity in the size of round towers. Most of them have a circumference of around 1.5 metres at the base while the wall is a metre thick. The position and scale of the doors, windows and storeys also follow broadly similar patterns.

The round tower of Kinneigh differs from every other building of that type to be found in Ireland, in as much as it presents a hexagonal base rising to halfway up the first floor. The floors are supported by flagstones projecting inwards towards the centre of the tower. The doorway and other openings are square headed and display

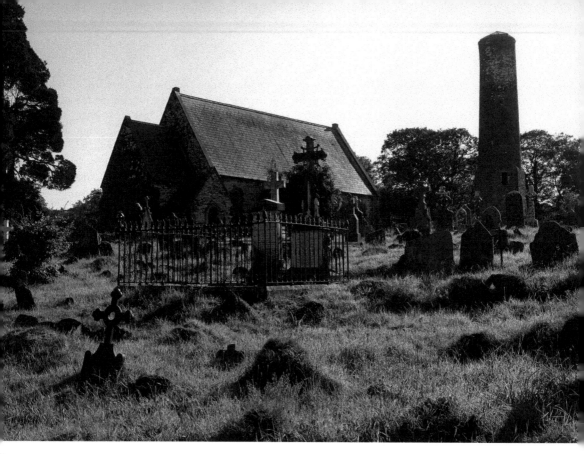

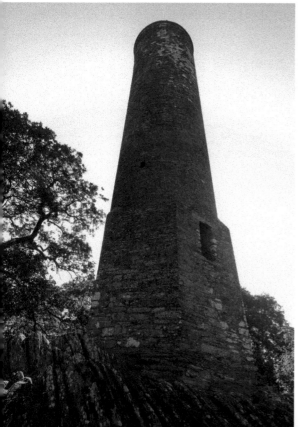

Above: Kinneigh Church and graveyard with the round tower.

Left: Kinneigh Round Tower.

the inclined sides so characteristic of early Irish work. The conical roof and top apertures no longer exist, so that the tower, though at present measuring 70 feet in height, must originally have been considerably higher. The doorway is placed at the unusual distance of 12 feet from the ground. Kinneigh Tower is one of those which, according to tradition, was erected by the famous Goban Saor, a very celebrated Irish architect.

The tower is one of only two round towers in County Cork (the other in Cloyne in East Cork) and is one of seventy-three structures in Ireland. Many round towers were described as ecclesiastical bell towers and storage spaces.

Built in 1856, St Bartholomew's Church of Ireland is built on the site of an ancient monastery of which the imposing round tower is the only upstanding remains. The church is the third church on the site. The extant one was built in the Romanesque style and displays finely crafted window and door surrounds. The community used the round tower as a bell tower.

47. The Legacy of the O'Sullivan Beares – Carriganass Castle

Carriganass Castle is the remains of an imposing sixteenth-century tower and walled courtyard located on the north bank of the Ouvane River near the village of Kealkill. The structure was five storeys high with a central tower of over 50 feet. Each corner had a defence tower. Some of the battlements are still in position on the western wall. Only portions of the northern and southern walls of the tower still stand.

The story of the castle is linked to the rise and fall of the fortunes of the O'Sullivan Bere chieftains. The tower house was built by the O'Sullivan Bere chieftain, Dermot O'Sullivan, around 1540. It was located at the eastern end of the O'Sullivan Bere territory, the main castle being at Dunboy. Following Dermot's death in 1548, there was a struggle for leadership within the O'Sullivan clan, resulting eventually in a division of the territory between Owen O'Sullivan, who accepted a knighthood from Queen Elizabeth, his brother Philip and his nephew Donal Cam.

In 1587, Donal Cam challenged his uncle's title. This led to an agreement in which Donal got land west of Adrigole and Dunboy, and Owen all the land east to Bantry. Both Donal Cam and his uncle Owen would have occupied Carriganass for different periods. At the time, Munster was in turmoil with the Desmond Rebellion being put down by Henry VIII and later by Queen Elizabeth. Philip III of Spain sent military help to the Irish clans and this led to the Battle of Kinsale between the English forces under Mountjoy and the Spanish and Irish soldiers from Munster and Ulster clans. While Donal Cam was on the Irish side, his cousin Owen was on the English side. After the Battle of Kinsale, Donal Cam was supposed to have abducted his cousin Owen's wife and held her captive on Dursey Island.

In the late 1990s, the University of Ulster at Coleraine was involved in a research programme in Bantry Bay, examining the history and archaeology of the O'Sullivan Beare lordship and the recent excavation was undertaken as part of a training

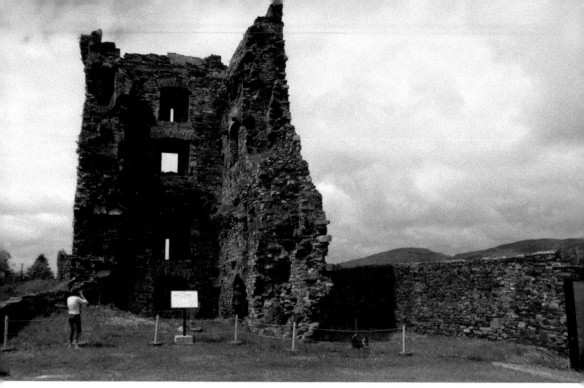

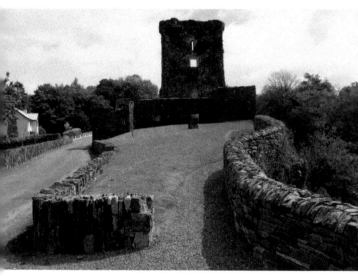

Above and left:
Carriganass Castle,
Keimaneigh.

programme for post-graduate maritime archaeology students. The Carriganass excavations produced some exciting results. They have shown that the site was attacked and abandoned in 1602 immediately prior to the siege of Dunboy. Evidence of this attack comes in the form of the collapsed masonry and violently destroyed stonework from the wall. Fragments of clay pipes are evidence of the last defenders protecting the site from attack. A quantity of animal and sheep bone, all of which had been butchered, was also found, giving an indication of the diet of the castle defenders and occupants.

Today Carriganass Castle Ltd oversees the maintenance and storytelling of the castle's history. The ruins of Carriganass stand as a fascinating place to visit.

48. In the Shadow of the Pass – Pass of Keimaneigh

The Pass of Keimaneigh is, by its very nature, a wild, rugged and natural boundary between the coastal regions of Bantry Bay in West Cork and the mountainous terrain which encompasses areas such as Gougane Barra and the upper River Lee valley. Over 3 kilometres long, the pass originated as a melt water channel from a melting glacier 20,000 years ago. On both sides of the pass are sheer cliffs rising each side to a height of 100 feet above the road. Today the pass marks the official division between the small Irish-speaking area of the West Cork/Gaeltacht and the rest of the region. In centuries gone by, it was the dividing territorial line between the Gaelic Irish families of the O'Sullivans and O'Learys.

The mountain pass is immortalised by local poet Máire Bhuí Ní Laoire in her poem 'Cath Céim An Fhia', an account of a battle in 1822 between Local Whiteboys and yeomen supported by British soldiers. A memorial exists in the middle of the pass, which recalls the conflict. It was economics not politics that determined the historic but tragic events. The Irish tenant farmer and the labourer experienced much economic hardship in 1810 and 1820s. A change in political system, nearly 180 years previously (1640s), had meant that many Irish landlords who chose not to be loyal to English government had their lands dispossessed and handed over to English gentry. The ensuing landlord systems, which strengthened and evolved in the eighteenth century, created rent increases for tenants and subsequent evictions for non-payment.

The local historical record of Iveleary for January 1822 recalls that the Keimaneigh area was used as a base for random attacks condemning rent oppression. Local folklore calls those men who gathered in the pass Rockites, rather than Whiteboys. The gathering in Keimaneigh was not unique and similar large groups of men were operating all over West Cork and elsewhere. One report of the time suggests that there were 2,000 men at Keimaneigh and 5,000 in the camps, which lay between Macroom and Millstreet. Those numbers are probably exaggerated, but the bands were obviously large.

The first incident in Keimaneigh took place during the night of 11 January 1822 when a party of around 500 Rockites raided a number of the homes of gentry in the Bantry area, looking for weapons. Achieving some success, they acquired a number of muskets, but no ammunition. The reaction by the gentry was instant and aggressive. The following day, Saturday 12th, Lord Bantry and his brother Captain White assembled a party of around fifty yeomanry and rode out in pursuit of the Rockites. The yeomanry were uniformed, mounted on horse and armed with sabres and pistols. Riding through the pass, they came upon the Rockites near Ballingeary but the latter rushed up into the hills and made back on foot for the pass. Realising the danger of their position, the yeomanry retreated back through the pass, avoiding the hail of stones hurled down from the heights. They then rode back to Bantry without achieving any victory from the foray.

By early February 1822, the Rockites abandoned their encampment in Keimaneigh and returned to their homes and farms. According to local lore, many members of

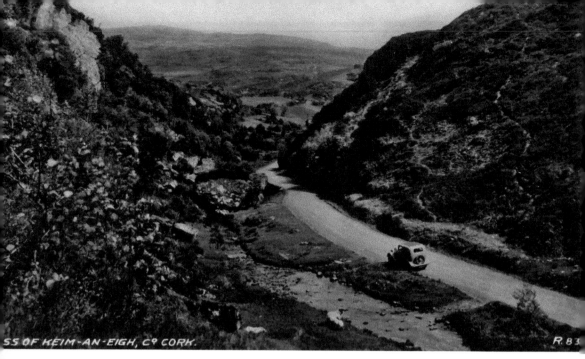

SS OF KEIM-AN-EIGH, Cº CORK.   R.83

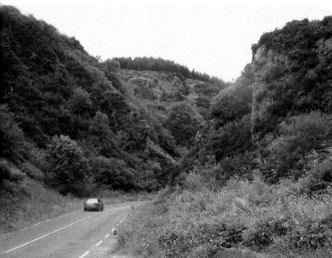

Above and left: Pass of Keimaneigh.

the group realised that they had made their protest and that there was not much more they could do. Their decisions may have been influenced by the thoughts of the reprisals, which did follow. In addition, it was most likely cold and wet in the winter of 1822 and there would have been a shortage of food. Local lore suggests that the actual number of Rockites killed was anything up to twelve people. Reprisals did take place. Lord Wellesley, the Lord Lieutenant in Cork City, set up a special commission to try the large number of prisoners taken at several affrays in Carriganimma, Deshure, Newmarket and at Keimaneigh. Altogether thirty-six men were sentenced to be hanged.

49. Finbarre's Rocky Place – Gougane Barra

Irish folklore has it that the patron saint of Cork, Finbarre, was educated as a monk and hence established several churches in the Munster area. One of these monastic sites was located on a rocky island in the centre of a lake overlooked by the Shehy Mountains where the River Lee rises. Indeed, the name of this lake today reflects the latter: 'Gougane Barra' or 'Finbarre's rocky place'.

Centuries later, the original and reputed monastery of St Finbarre was to become ruinous and Fr Denis O' Mahony built a replica of it around 1700. The buildings that Fr O'Mahony built – i.e. the Pilgrim's Terrace and Church – still survive and have been altered through time to preserve them. Fr C. M. O'Brien's book on the *Life of St Finbarr,* possibly published to coincide with the dedication of the oratory, seems to serve as some kind of official guidebook to the oratory. He notes that St Finbarre's Oratory (built *c.* 1900/01) owes its origin to the local parish priest Fr Patrick Hurley who obtained financing for the erection of the oratory from two wealthy Irish Americans in America (one living in Chicago). The new oratory replaced Fr Denis O'Mahony's near two-hundred-year-old ruinous oratory.

The design of the church is bound with the Gaelic revival of the late nineteenth century. That was a time when there was a resurgence of interest in engaging with the Gaelic language and ancient Irish folklore, sports, songs, architecture and arts were considered to be part of the pre-English conquest heritage of the native Irish people. The oratory is built in Hiberno-Byzantine style and modelled after the Chapel of Cormac on the Rock of Cashel (begun in AD 1127).

Mr Samuel F. Hynes, Cork, designed St Finbarr's Oratory and the artist was Mr M. J. C. Buckley, Cork and Bruges, Belgium. Samuel F. Hynes was part of a wider group of late nineteenth-century architects employed to create new symbolism for the Roman Catholic Church, which was growing in strength since the sanctioning of the Catholic Emancipation Act in 1829.

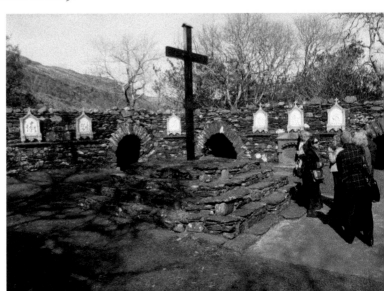

Pilgrimage cells, Gougane Barra.

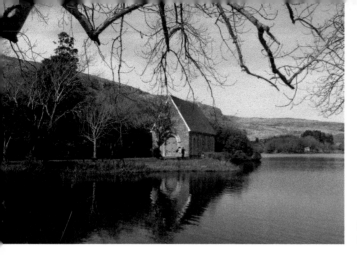

St Finbarr's Oratory,
Gougane Barra.

As for Michael J. C. Buckley, he was of Irish birth. He seems to have been in business on his own until around 1881 when he became a partner of Cox & Son. After the firm was bought out in the 1890s, Buckley appears to have returned to Ireland and continued to work. The walling is of mountain stone and is relieved by dressings of limestone, while the roof, like the Chapel of Cormac, was originally of stone, necessitated by the heavy rains that prevail in mountain districts. Revd C. M. O'Brien's book *Life of St Finbarr* (c. 1901) notes that the western end of Gougane Oratory is ornamented by a boldly excised doorway of limestone, with hook shafts and caps and vases, the arches being enriched with chevron ornament. At the head of the label mould is a boldly cut head of St Finbarre. The original plan was to have a round tower at the entrance to the oratory, but it was never completed.

50. Ireland's First National Park – Gougane Barra

In 1960, the national element of Gougane Barra was once again invested in when it was chosen as Ireland's first national park. In the late 1950s, plans were drawn up to open up some of Ireland's particularly attractive forest blocks as national forest parks. Up to that point in time, investment in state forests amounted to £22.5 million. The investment aimed to achieve maximum utilisation of the land, that patches of land, which could not be used economically for pasture or tillage, could be devoted to timber production. The forestry division in 1963 provided direct employment for 4,500 men, 330 of whom were employed in Cork and Kerry forests. In 1963, the state planting rate was 25,000 acres per annum.

Apart from the economic advantages, the state also sought to improve local scenery affected by forestry plantations. In this light, it was decided to develop a number of national parks, providing new recreational facilities and contributing to the development of the tourist industry. The idea of opening the forest to the public was first put forward by Colonel Roland H. Packwood, who was engaged as a consultant to the Irish Forestry Division in 1937. He formed the idea from his experience with the British Forestry Commission, in which he served as Chief

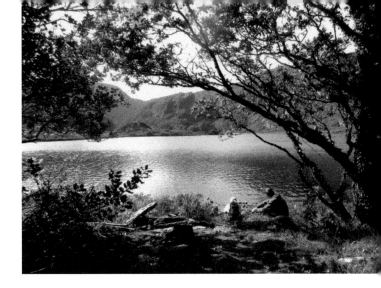

Gougane Barra Lake.

Engineer. Gougane Barra in County Cork and the Derrybawn and Lugduff properties of Glendalough were selected as the first two areas of development, or the Republic's first forest parks. A grant was secured in September 1960 to create a new road into the heart of Gougane's forestry scheme.

A visit by an *Irish Independent* journalist in early 1962 noted of the area's history:

> In a recent visit we left the unfinished road and climbed further up the mountain to a spot where one can straddle the famous river, one foot on each bank. This place has a niche in history. The road at another point passes at the base of a deep ravine. It had been seen by few people because of its previous inaccessibility. Known locally as Poll, or the Black Glen, it was used once by the West Cork Flying Column in their famous trek to avoid encirclement by British forces during the War of Independence. The column led by famed Tom Barry, was being confined in the valley of Coomhola on the Kerry side of the mountains. A British pincer movement was an all-out drive to smash the fighting men of West Cork. All escape routes were cut off. A local guide led the column in a night escape across treacherous, boggy land.

Gougane Barra Forest Park was officially opened by Micheál Ó Móráin, Minister for Lands, on 20 September 1966.

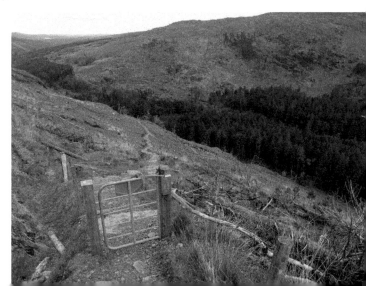

Gougane Forest park.

About the Author

For over twenty years, Kieran has actively promoted Cork's heritage with its various communities and people. He has led and continues to lead successful heritage initiatives through his community talks, city and county school heritage programmes, walking tours, newspaper articles, books and his work through his heritage consultancy business. For the past twenty years, Kieran has written a local heritage column in the *Cork Independent* on the history, geography and their intersection with modern-day life in communities in Cork City and County. He holds a PhD in Geography from the National University of Ireland Cork and has interests in ideas of landscape, collective memory, narrative and identity structures. Kieran is the author of twenty-two local history books. In June 2009, May 2014 and May 2019 Kieran was elected as a local government councillor (Independent) to Cork City Council. He is also a member of the European Committee of the Regions. More on Kieran's work can be viewed at www.corkheritage.ie and www.kieranmccarthy.ie.

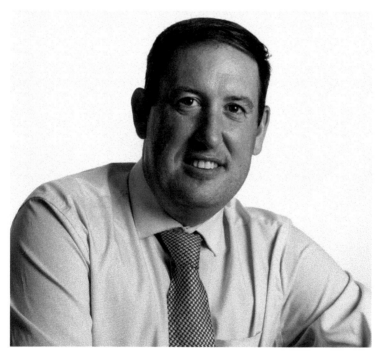